For Lucy and Fiep
Who brought us together

Concept   Jur Baart
Text   Bas Korpel
Illustrations   Jur Baart
Photography   Danny Griffioen
Publisher   BIS Publishers

BURP
THE
OTHER
WINE
BOOK

NTRODUCTION

There is a story behind every wine. As a winemaker, you can
make a statement with your label. It is the showcase of your
company. And more importantly, it can persuade consumers to buy
your product. The label should be in line with the wine you can
expect in your glass. And that's why we decided to make this
book: because we strongly believe that a wine tastes better when
you know the story behind it.

Just like folk tales, the stories behind the wine are often
passed on — and sometimes spiced up in the retelling. Rest
assured that this also happened with the stories in this book.

Although we regularly describe the expected taste of the wines we
selected for this book, taste was not a criterion for us, only
a pleasant side effect. After all, taste is debatable and there
are already enough publications that judge a wine's flavour.
We therefore selected 40 wines, each with a distinct label and a
matching story.

Our selection did not focus on the vinification techniques of
the wines. What is striking, however, is the exceptionally high
proportion of natural wines. Apparently, this group of winemakers
(in some cases new to the profession) is paying more attention to
how their products find their way to the consumer. Yet Burp also
includes a number of all-time classics that should not be missed
— essential not only in this book, but also in your wine cellar.

We hope Burp will give you lots of new stories to tell while
drinking your next bottle of wine.

Enjoy reading. Cheers. Burp!

INDEX

CHATEAU
COS
D'ESTOURNEL

Saint-Estèphe AOC, France

THE MAHARAJAH OF SAINT ESTEPHE

The story of Château Cos d'Estournel is
the story of a man named Louis-Gaspard
d'Estournel. He inherited the land and
was the first to identify its exceptional
quality. A Cos (the 's' is not silent)
is a small hill consisting mainly of a
pebbly soil. In 1811, he planted his land
with vines and named the chateau after
himself. Louis-Gaspard was a horse trader
with a thriving business in Arabian
steeds. He often went abroad for work,
visiting Arab countries and travelling
through Africa and India.

Louis-Gaspard d'Estournel was outgoing,
innovative and lavish in his spending.
If there would be one Little Britain
character to compare him with, it would
be Daffyd Thomas and his catchphrase
'I'm the only gay in the village'. As a
result of his travels, the exterior and
interior of Cos d'Estournel is a blend of
African, Arabic and Indian influences.
It is said that the expertly carved
wooden door at the main entrance to the
chateau was imported from the Sultan of
Zanzibar's palace. This and many other
works of art, including the oriental
pagodas adorning the chateau's towers
earned him the nickname 'the Maharajah of
Saint-Estèphe'.

A WELL TRAVELLED WINE

Unlike many of the other Bordeaux producers, Louis-Gaspard d'Estournel did not sell his wines with the help of a go-between known as a *négociant* or trader. Why should he? More often than not, he used his wine as currency to purchase his beloved horses. Travelling by ship, he brought along barrels of his own wine and exchanged it for stallions. On one of his trips to India, he was unable to offload all of his barrels and had to bring some of them back home. Oddly enough, the wines seemed to have improved in quality. He labelled them with an 'R' — returned from India — and quickly noticed a spike in demand.

From that moment on, all of his wines were shipped to travel from Bordeaux and back again. Their ties to exotic destinations grew even closer. In the meantime, the chateau had become an exotic landmark within the village of Saint-Estèphe, a role it still retains today. Prominent wine producers in Bordeaux frequently display the chateau on the label. The Château Cos d'Estournel label is classic, timeless, yet exceptionally distinctive.

FOR BITTER FOR SWEET

So how did it end up for our friend Louis-Gaspard? He lived beyond his means, ended up broke, and unfortunately had to sell his life's work – that means the chateau – in 1852. A year later, he passed away at the ripe old age of 91, sans all possessions after a life of luxury. The question is whether we should feel sorry for him...

The estate was sold to Charles Cecil Martyn, a businessman from London who had been living in Paris. Under his supervision, the estate received the widespread acclaim that Louis-Gaspard had been seeking all his life. Château Cos d'Estournel was included as a Second Growth in the classification of 1855. The wines of Cos d'Estournel are still classified as Deuxième Grand Cru Classé to this day.

COS D'E

GRAND VIN DE BORDEAUX

The pebbled soil of the hill is the key success factor of Cos d'Estournel, offering ideal conditions for vines to grow long roots to get their nutrients. About 65% of the land is planted with cabernet sauvignon. The second most frequently planted grape is merlot at 33%. The remaining 2% are equally divided between cabernet franc and petit verdot.

The Grand Vin is a blend that changes every year, depending on the quality of the grapes. Cos d'Estournel also makes a second wine named after the towers of the chateau: Pagodes de Cos. Château Cos d'Estournel is a long-lived Saint-Estèphe that peaks after 15-20 years.

GAJA
CAMARCANDA
PROMIS

Toscana IGT, Italy

ANGELO GAJA

Pioneer, visionary, enfant terrible: this Barbaresco-based winemaker is all these and more. But his success is undeniable! It was Angelo Gaja (1940) himself who made Piemonte's wines among the most sought-after in the world. His family winery is based in Barbaresco, the area where winemakers are legally required to use the noble nebbiolo grape. Barbaresco is often mentioned together with Barolo. These top-notch wine regions are also known as the King and Queen of Piemonte – with Barbaresco viewed as the queen due to its relatively soft touch.

Gaja has vineyards in both Barbaresco and Barolo, although you would not necessarily find those names on all its wines. Angelo Gaja ignores local rules and legislation in favour of the ultimate flavour of his wines. From 1996 to 2012 he chose to add a dash of barbera to his single vineyard Barbaresco wines. As a result, he had to declass his best wines and market them under the less famous Langhe DOC.

THE ROAD TO TUSCANY

Gaja is more than Piemonte alone; the Gaja family purchased two estates in Tuscany. In 1994, they bought Pieve Santa Restituta where Gaja produces Brunello di Montalcino — always made from 100% sangiovese. And in 1996 Angelo Gaja finally became the proud owner of an estate in Bolgheri named after the endless negotiations: Ca'Marcanda. With its maritime climate along the Tuscan coast, this region is the perfect place to grow Bordeaux grapes such as merlot, cabernet sauvignon and cabernet franc. In the past, wines made from these grapes had to be declassified to the level of a simple table wine. This gave way to the introduction of Super Tuscans, with the most famous examples being Tignanello, Sassicaia and Ornellaia.

Now that Angelo Gaja has wineries in Piemonte and Tuscany, he rides up and down the Italian highway on a weekly basis. The drive from Barbaresco to Ca'Marcanda is 384 kilometres, and he feels that he has truly arrived in Tuscany when driving down a road surrounded by cypresses, the tall trees that are characteristic of the region. This image of Tuscany is reflected on all the Ca'Marcanda wine labels.

Promis

Angelo Gaja arrives in Tuscany

THE PROMISE

Gaja produces four different wines at Ca'Marcanda: three reds and a white. The sole white, *Vistamare*, is made from vermentino, viognier and fiano. The entry-level red known as *Promis* – literally 'the promise' – is made from young vines of merlot, syrah and sangiovese. Promis provides an excellent example of the future potential of these new vines. This wine is pleasant to drink fairly young, especially with tomato-based pasta dishes due to the strong sangiovese contribution.

The black-labelled *Magari* is the next level: a Bordeaux blend of cabernet franc, cabernet sauvignon and petit verdot. Finally, the winery's flagship wine is called *Camarcanda*, a stunning blend of merlot, cabernet sauvignon and cabernet franc. It's a textbook Bordeaux with a Tuscan twist.

Angelo Gaja surrounded by his family

TOO BAD...

Angelo Gaja entered the family business in 1961 at the age of 21. As a form of damage control, his father made him responsible 'only' for the work in the vineyard. However, Gaja realised he had to make a statement to be noticed in the international world of fine wines, which was dominated by cabernet sauvignon at that time. He decided to take out all of his nebbiolo plants in his family's finest vineyard, Bricco, and replace them with cabernet sauvignon.

His father Giovanni was not amused, mumbling *'darmagi'* (local dialect for 'what a shame') and shaking his head every time he passed his once-beloved vineyard. Young Angelo had his revenge, though: he produced a 100% cabernet sauvignon from Barbaresco that — of course — needed to be declassified to the level of Langhe DOC. That wine is still produced every year under the name Darmagi.

ENATE
CHARDONNAY
FERMENTADO
EN BARRICA

DO Somontano, Spain

AT THE FOOT OF THE MOUNTAINS

What do the Italian region of Piemonte and Somontano have in common? In both regions, it's the local word for 'at the foot of the mountain'. In the case of Somontano, we find ourselves by the Pyrenees in the province of Huesca. This Denominación de Origen was created in 1984, and Bodegas Enate was founded shortly after in 1992.

At Enate they grow chardonnay and gewürztraminer for their five different white wines and tempranillo, cabernet sauvignon, merlot and syrah for their ten different red wines. The winery also makes a bold, dark cabernet sauvignon rosado, far distant from the pale 'Rosé de Provence' wines that are so common these days — bucking the trend in colour, and even including some tannin structure.

STIRRED NOT SHAKEN

Three different wines featuring 100% chardonnay are produced at Enate. The entry-level Chardonnay 234 is named after the block where the grapes are from. The top-level Uno Chardonnay receives a tailor-made vinification depending on the characteristics of the vintage. This Chardonnay Fermentado en Barrica has been there from the start in 1992 and is considered one of the flagship wines of the bodega.

Both alcoholic and malolactic fermentation take place on new French oak barrels, hence the name 'Fermentado en Barrica'. In this process, first the grape juice turns into wine, and the malic acid is transformed into a softer-tasting lactic acid. In terms of taste, this wine goes directly from green apple to buttery tones. And there you have the difference between (basic) Chablis and Meursault... During the next seven months, as it matures in oak barrels, the wine is left in contact with its 'lees' or dead yeast cells. Every other week, a bâtonnage takes place, which means that the lees are stirred through the wine. The result is rich, creamy and exotic.

Chardonnay Fermentado en Barrica

Enate

THE UNPREDICTABILITY OF NATURE

Antonio Saura

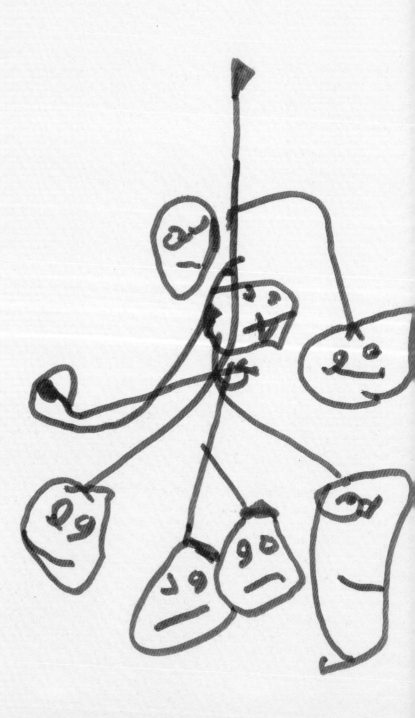

From the very start, Enate wanted to embrace modern art and see it as the essence of its identity. Each Enate wine label is enriched with a unique work of art. Reflecting that deliberate identity, Enate is not only a winemaker. It's also a museum housing all sixteen original artworks that were made for the labels of the different wines produced at the estate. The idea behind this is the contrast between the mathematical precision of the winemaker and the unpredictability of the artist. It reminds us that winemakers also have to make the best of the natural conditions of the vintage.

The Enate labels are always a single piece and provide key information in braille as well. The artwork on the Chardonnay Fermentado en Barrica is entitled 'Bunch with Seven Grapes', a piece by Antonio Saura from 1993. This was the first wine to be released after the launch in 1992, and therefore also the first artwork created for Bodegas Enate.

A PAINTER NOT AN ARTIST

Antonio Saura (1930-1998) was a logical choice as the first artist to grace Enate's labels. Born in the city of Huesca, near the bodega in Somontano, Saura made the drawing for Enate towards the end of his life, after a career that included exhibitions in Madrid, Barcelona, New York, Paris, Munich and Amsterdam. His favourite colours were black, more black, grey and brown. Saura's style was dark and would have been perfect for the album cover of any hard rock band.

In his own lifetime, Saura wanted to be known as an artist so badly that he even listed himself as 'Antonio Saura, painter' in the local telephone book – prompting frequent phone calls from people asking if he could paint their house. He has gained some degree of posthumous fame, since a Madrid metro station has been named after him. *'Próxima Estación: Antonio Saura.'*

CHATEAU
MOUTON
ROTHSCHILD

AOC Pauillac, France

DIFFERENT LABEL EACH YEAR

Château Mouton Rothschild produces one Grand Vin each year, changing the image on their label every time. They have been doing this since 1945 – an outstanding vintage, as it happens – and Mouton Rothschild 1945 is still one of the most sought-after wines in the world today. The label bears a 'V' and the words '1945 Année de la Victoire', celebrating the end of World War II.

In the early years, the artists who designed the labels were close personal friends of Baron Philippe de Rothschild: Jean Hugo (1946), Jean Cocteau (1947) and Léonor Fini (1952). Later they were followed by some of the greatest artists of our time: Salvador Dalí (1958), Marc Chagall (1970), Wassily Kandinsky (1971), Pablo Picasso (1973), Andy Warhol (1975), Keith Haring (1988), Karel Appel (1994), Prince Charles (2004) – that's right, the Prince of Wales – and Jeff Koons (2010).

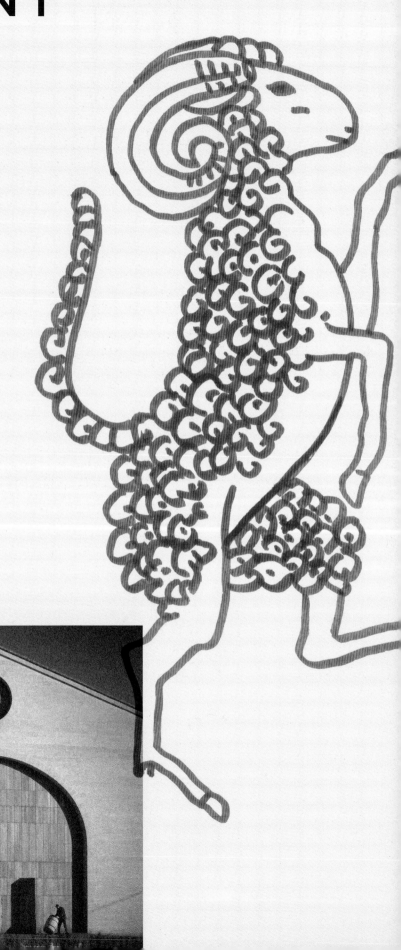

NINETEEN EIGHTY NINE 'DIE MAUER'

Georg Baselitz, East German by birth, is a controversial painter and sculptor known for his disruptive, inverted artworks; he has been turning his images upside down since 1969. In the year that the Berlin Wall fell, there was no better artist imaginable for the 1989 vintage label. Baselitz created 'Die Mauer', reflecting how that historic event turned the world upside down. His artwork includes the words *Drüben sein jetzt hier*: 'Over there is now over here'.

According to Mouton Rothschild each artist is given complete freedom to design their artwork for the label. The 1993 label designed by Polish-French modern artist Balthus was rejected for US import by the Bureau of Alcohol, Tobacco and Firearms because of his pencil drawing of a nude. The 1993 Mouton Rothschild for the US market was labelled with a blank space instead, quickly becoming a collectors' item. Rumour has it that the artist receives 24 cases of his 'own' wine upon completion. Too bad for Pablo Picasso, who died in April 1973, not long after delivering his artwork for that year's vintage.

HISTORY OF MOUTON ROTHSCHILD

Mayer Amschel Rothschild, of the English Rothschilds, sent five of his sons across Europe in the late 18th century to establish powerful financial institutions. His son Baron Nathaniel de Rothschild acquired the property in 1853, and the estate is still family owned today. In 1922, at the age of 20, Baron Philippe de Rothschild decided to devote his entire life to the estate. Even after her mother died in 1945 in the Ravensbrück concentration camp, his daughter (and only child) Baronne Philippine de Rothschild continued his work. Since her death in 2014, the estate has been in the hands of her three children: Camille, Philippe and Julien.

Château Mouton Rothschild currently owns 84 hectares of vines in Pauillac planted with 80% cabernet sauvignon, 16% merlot, 3% cabernet franc and 1% petit verdot. The assemblage of the Grand Vin changes every year in order to create the best wine possible from that year's harvest.

PREMIER

The winery's motto is *Mouton ne change*: 'Mouton does not change'. It may seem odd, but there's a history behind it. Until 1973 the motto was: *Premier ne puis, second ne daigne, Mouton suis*: 'First I cannot be, second is below my dignity, I am Mouton'. After more than fifty years of intensive lobbying, the classification was finally changed from Second to Premier Cru Classé — the highest rank, which had been reserved exclusively for Château Lafite Rothschild, Château Latour, Château Margaux and Château Haut-Brion. From that moment on, the official motto became *Premier je suis, second je fus, Mouton ne change*: 'First I am, second I was, Mouton does not change'.

Interestingly, Château Mouton Rothschild is the only estate that has managed to change its classification. The upgrade — or 'rectification', as Mouton prefers — was signed by the French Minister of Agriculture, an ambitious 41-year-old man who became Prime Minister ('Premier' in French) the year after. In 1995 he became the President of France. His name? Jacques Chirac.

WEINGUT KNOLL
GRUNER
VELTLINER
FEDERSPIEL

Wachau, Austria

SAINT ALCOHOL

It is hard to forget the first time you drink a bottle of Knoll. Not only because of the wine. It's mainly because of the impressive baroque-style label. At Knoll they produce 23 different wines per year, originating from distinctive vineyards and made from different grape varieties. Each and every bottle bears the image of Saint Urban of Langres. He was the sixth bishop of Langres (situated near Dijon and Burgundy) during the 4th century. As the patron saint of winemakers, he is said to offer protection from frost, hailstorms, blight and, not unimportantly, alcoholism.

Apart from St Urban himself, there is a poem on the label, scripted on either side of the saint in gothic letters. The bisected lines of the stanza read:

Tut mir nur den   *Wein nicht taufen*
Lasst ihn doch als   *Heiden laufen*
Nur der Durst   *soll christlich sein*
So erweist man   *Ehr dem Wein*

Roughly translated, it means something like: 'Do not baptise the wine for me. Let it run as a heathen. Only thirst should be Christian. This is how one honours wine.'

In 1983, producers from the Wachau established their own association. The Vinea Wachau now has over 200 members that collectively own over 85% of the land in the region. They not only follow Austrian wine laws, but also have their own standards. Their regional designations include Steinfeder, Federspiel and Smaragd.

The Steinfeder wines are the lightest, named after the feathery grass that often grows on the rocky local hillsides.

Named for a lizard's brilliant emerald colour, the Smaragd wines are considered the top range of the Wachau and can age up to 20 years. Federspiel references a long-distant chapter in Wachau history when falconry was a favourite pastime. The Weingut Knoll Grüner Veltliner Federspiel is an all-time classic. Almost as traditional in taste as its own label, the wine boasts a racy acidity and clear minerality, with notes of ripe apple, juicy pear and a hint of freshly ground white pepper.

OBERLEUTNANT SIEGFRIED STOITZNER

The label bears an image of a painting that is in the possession of the Knoll family. The painter's signature can be seen on the label in the left corner, below one of the angels: Siegfried Stoitzner (1892-1976). This Austrian painter and publisher of art postcards came from an artistic family; his father and brother were painters as well. In World War I, he volunteered for the army and returned a senior lieutenant or *Oberleutnant*.

In 1919, he was the founding member of the Wachau Artists Association. Joining the Society of Fine Artists in Vienna in 1941; he seemed the type of man who enjoyed such memberships. After World War II, however, he was expelled from the Vienna society due to his dubious affiliations: he had also been a member of the Austrian wing of the German Nazi Party.

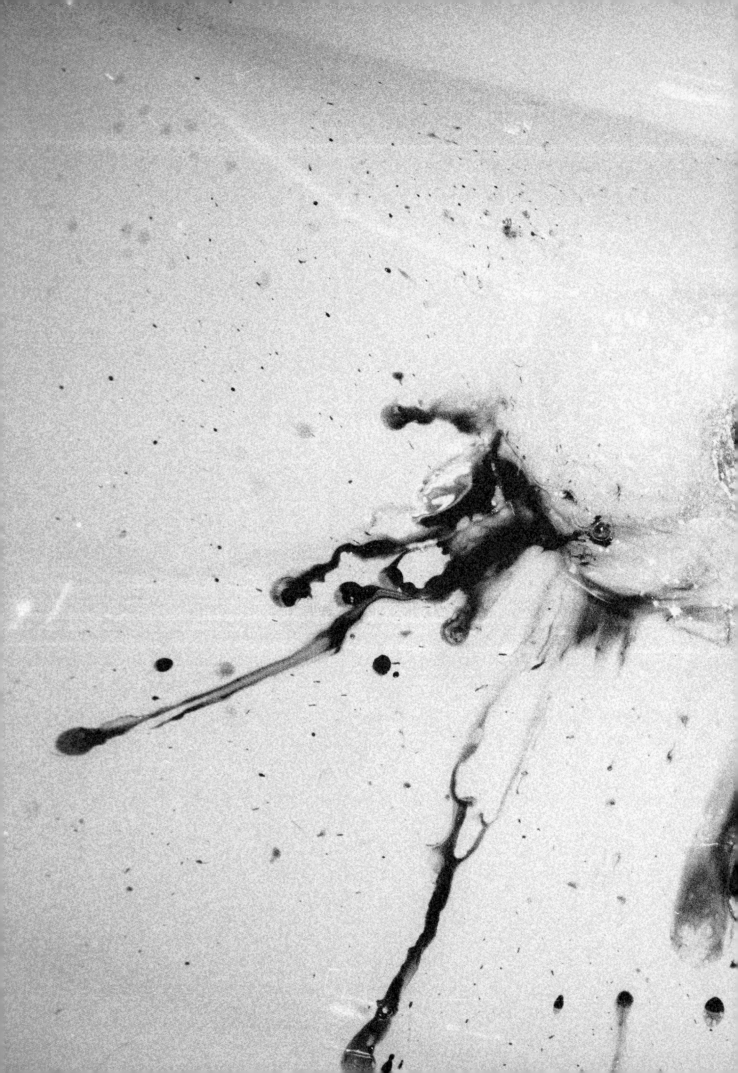

GUT
OGGAU
THEODORA
(WHITE)

Burgenland, Austria

AUSTRIAN DYNASTY

The name Gut Oggau comes from a small
Austrian town situated on the banks of
Lake Neusiedl: Oggau am Neusiedler See.
Oggau produces a whole family of wines —
to be more precise, three grandchildren,
five parents and two grandparents. The
characters of the wines are connected to
the family members.

You can imagine that the grandparents'
wines — *Mechtild* (white) and *Bertholdi*
(red) — are single vineyard wines made
from old vines grown on a soil rich
in schist and limestone. A 200-year-
old wine press is used to produce these
wines, which have a lot to tell. The
parent wines' all have characters that
can be related to the family members:
Josephine (red) is easy-going and open to
strangers. *Timoteus* (white) is strong,
powerful and balanced, where *Joschuari*
(red) is charismatic and complex. His
wife *Wiltrude* (sweet) is attractive,
playful and exotic, while 'uncle'
Emmeram (gewürztraminer) seems to have
a phenomenal effect on women.

The wines of the youngest generation come from a gravelly soil. They are bold, straightforward and exceptionally popular. The range of grandchildren include a white (*Theodora*), red (*Atanasius*) and of course a rosé: *Winifred*.

When it comes to the young, cheerful and attractive *Theodora* (white), the family plot thickens. Theodora is the daughter of Wiltrude, who had a short but passionate affair with 'uncle' Emmeram, the brother of her husband Joschuari. Theodora has a strong relationship with her beloved grandmother Mechtild and her favourite uncle Emmeram. The latter still firmly believes himself to be Theodora's father.

All the biodynamic wines of Gut Oggau are fully Demeter-certified. The estate works with the black grape varieties blaufränkisch and zweigelt. The white wines are made from grüner veltliner, welschriesling, weissburgunder and gewürztraminer.

Theodora is a blend of grüner veltliner and welschriesling, fermented and aged in large oak barrels. It can be considered a natural wine, as it is unfiltered and no extra sulphur is added. Shaking the bottle before consumption gives an extra dimension when drinking the wine. Expect the taste of Jonagold, honeydew, champagne-ish yeast notes and freshly ground white pepper. Typical for grüner veltliner in general.

The owners: Eduard and Stephanie Tscheppe-Eselböck

NOT SO SWEET FAMILY REUNION

The family members of Gut Oggau offer a wide range of possibilities, for instance when wines with different personalities are blended. In the difficult vintage of 2016, this was the case: instead of ten wines, Gut Oggau only made four. The result was a family reunion. On the label, the faces of several family members were merged into a single visage. And how about a year when botrytis does not occur on Wiltrude's vines? When that happens, the 'Wiltrude Süss' is no longer sweet at all. Also new in the portfolio of Gut Oggau are the Maskerade wines, mysterious field blends from vineyards they recently took over. The new faces on the labels are literally wearing masks,

as the winemakers have not yet discovered the person behind the mask.

Eduard and Stephanie Tscheppe-Eselböck are the owners of Gut Oggau, although they themselves do not occupy a place in the family tree. Their packaging was designed by Vienna-based creative agency 'Jung von Matt'. They even make tiny differences to the images on the labels every year to make the faces look a bit older for every vintage. Their design was rewarded with a Gold Lion in Cannes. But are they only responsible for the design, or do they also play a role in the amazing story-telling of this wine estate...?

Theodora (White)

Gut Oggau

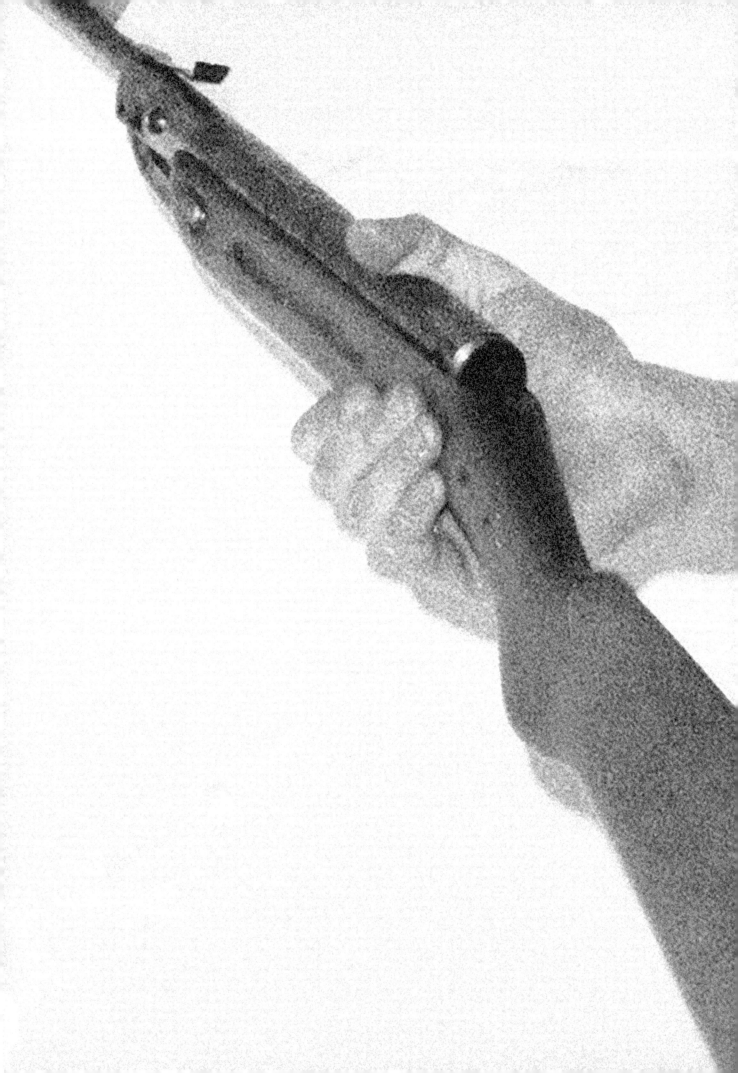

RATTI
BATTAGLIONE

Barbera d'Alba DOC, Italy

THE GREAT INNOVATOR OF BAROLO

From the castle of Barolo to the famous village of La Morra is a 10-minute drive by scooter. On your way you'll pass Cantina Renato Ratti, named after the great innovator of Barolo. Nowadays the domain is in the hands of the second-generation winemaker Pietro Ratti. In the 1960s, his father bought the Abbey of the Annunciation, where he founded his winery. Where the abbey first housed Benedictine monks, later accommodating Italian troops in World War II, today it is used as a private wine museum.

Renato Ratti had visited Burgundy, where he was inspired to make single vineyard wines. Before then, it had been quite common to make Barolo as a blend from different vineyards. Ratti created a map where he distinguished different crus, very much like in Burgundy. In 1965 he created his first single vineyard Barolo: Marcenasco. The wine didn't even mention the name of Barolo on the front label. Just like every Grand Cru in Burgundy, it only displayed the name of the vineyard. Other producers in the region soon followed him in making single vineyard wines.

Piemonte is a wealthy Italian region with a long and embattled history of disputed authority. The Italian word 'Battaglione' literally means 'battalion'. The soldier on the label wears a historic Piemontese uniform from 1793, the year of the Battle of Saorgio, where two French armies faced the troops of the Kingdom of Sardinia. In those days, Piemonte was part of the Kingdom of Sardinia and therefore fell under the reign of King Vittorio Amadeo – known internationally as Victor Amadeus III, the Duke of Savoy.

Back in 1562, Emanuel Philibert of the House of Savoy had made Turin the capital of their empire. When the island was annexed in 1720, Turin became the capital city of the Kingdom of Sardinia. The soldiers in traditional uniform on the Ratti labels are a nod to the geographical location where the grapes come from. The Piemontese won the Battle of Saorgio in 1793, but the borders have shifted again since then. A quick look at the map shows that Saorgio has been located in France since 1860, and is now called Saorge.

THE RATTI FAMILY

Before starting his own winery in Piemonte, Renato Ratti started his professional career in the wine business in São Paolo. During his years in Brazil, he worked for the global vermouth brand Cinzano.

Renato Ratti died unexpectedly at the age of 54, leaving his son Pietro with no choice but to take over his position at the tender age of 22. He has been in charge of the winery named after his famous father ever since.

MOTIF VERMOUTH WHITE

Styria, Austria

EYE
CANDY

'There is joy. With a smile on your face, the world looks completely different.' These phrases may sound very much like a horoscope, but it is actually the description of this fortified wine. Vermouth from Austria, white and sweet, with Alpine botanicals, and made from grapes that flourish in the Illyrian climate. We are in Styria, or *Steiermark*, as the Austrians call their federal state.

Motif Wines are fine art in purest form. They make table wines that go by names in local dialect: Gschekat, Gschniglt, Wax, Dign and Bixgrod. Their origin, grape varieties or vinification methods are one big mystery, but each and every bottle design is sheer eye candy, a delight to behold. The range of vermouth wines consists of a red, white and rosé. Motif Wines is a brand of Weingut Muster Gamlitz.

WITHOUT PREJUDICE PLEASE

'Life often is too complex to think too much about it. Let thoughts go, take a deep breath, inhale life.' Is that René Descartes, Jean-Paul Sartre or Confucius? No, it's Motif Wines! This producer no longer dictates what you see, taste or smell; all they do (and they do it well) is provide a design that will help you understand the drink in your glass. The name Motif means pattern, design or recurring theme.

All the labels used by Motif Wines are made by En Garde, a brand agency specialised in digital media and design. En Garde is located in Graz, the provincial capital of Styria. Their starting point was to create an unprejudiced environment that provides a counter-note to the existing values within the wine world. By the looks of the wines, they succeeded in their undertaking.

Vermouth White

Motif

IS
IT
GIN

Giacomo Casanova

The taste of the Vermouth White is reminiscent of a gin and tonic. But is it really gin that we're tasting? More accurately, it has the taste of the mixer: tonic! To be more precise: it bears the distinctive tang of quinine, the ingredient in tonic water that gives it its bitter flavour. Quinine comes from the bark of the cinchona tree and was also used as an anti-malaria agent. This explains the incredible success of gin & tonic in the former British colony of India and the brand name Bombay Sapphire.

Apart from quinine, many different Alpine botanicals have been added to the fortified wine, giving it distinct notes of gentian and marjoram. It's floral, very herbaceous and medicinal with liquorice root, minty tones and eucalyptus, but also citrus, and spices such as star anise. You can drink this Vermouth on its own, but it's more common to use it in a cocktail or mixer.

I AM NOT YOUR CASANOVA

Vermouth was first made in the 18th century, inspired by a fortified German wine flavoured with absinthe — a drink once known as wormwood. The German word for it is 'Wermut', which is where we get the name vermouth. The world's most famous vermouth is Martini. The other big Italian brand is Cinzano, originating from 1757 and considered to be the favourite drink of Giacomo Casanova: Italian adventurer, writer and notorious womaniser… but also known as the Jeffrey Epstein of his century.

Casanova has his own cocktail named after him, and you can make it with Motif as well. Fill a tumbler glass with pureed strawberries, lime juice and sugar. Pour a shot of Motif Vermouth White on top, and garnish with a strawberry. Other mixed drinks that do very well with this include the *Motif Vermouth White & Tonic* or the *Motif Spritz* with prosecco and soda.

CHATEAU
LEOVILLE
POYFERRE

AOC Saint-Julien, France

THE HISTORY OF LÉOVILLE

The history of Château Léoville Poyferré starts in the year 1638. At that time, the land was owned by a member of the Bordeaux parliament, Jean de Moytie, who called his estate Mont-Moytie. It is one of the first estates in the Médoc to produce wines, along with Château Margaux and the estate that we know today as Château Latour. In 1722 Blaise-Antoine-Alexandre de Gascq, Lord of Léoville married the man's daughter, Jeanne de Moytie, and became the new owner of the estate – and in 1740 he renamed it after himself: Léoville.

There was a time when the Léoville property sprawled across the region, one-third the size of all the vineyards of Saint Julien. When Blaise de Gascq died in the mid-1770s the estate covered 120 hectares, making it the largest vineyard in the Médoc. Blaise and Jeanne died childless, passing their estate to their three nephews and niece. One of them left the country in 1794, at the height of the French Revolution. His land was separated from the main Léoville estate and became Château Léoville Barton. The rest was divided up after a family feud in 1840, splitting into Léoville Las Cases and Léoville Poyferré. The latter was named after Baron Jean-Marie Poyferré de Cerès, who married one of the heirs.

THE EMPEROR'S NEW CHATEAU

Just imagine: we have a huge domain with a chateau on it. What happens to the chateau if you divide the land? The chateau was divided between Léoville Poyferré and Léoville Las Cases, and in fact remains split to this day.

Léoville Barton had no problems at all with the new situation. The originally Irish family already owned the neighbouring domain of Langoa Barton, including its own chateau. To this day, the wines of Léoville Barton are made at Château Langoa Barton. In a certain sense, Château Léoville Barton can be seen as 'The Emperor's New Château'.

laise-Antoine-Alexandre de Gascq

FROM SIMPLE SKETCH TO BUILDING

When the current owners, the Cuvelier family, acquired Léoville Poyferré in 1920, they easily shared the chateau with Léoville Las Cases. The Cuvelier family were wine merchants, and owned (and still own) Château Le Crock Cru Bourgeois Exceptionnel in Saint-Estèphe.

But shouldn't a Bordeaux wine always show its chateau on the label? This must have crossed the minds of the Cuvelier family. Since the historic chateau was already depicted on the label of Léoville Las Cases, they made a simple sketch of a fictitious chateau, and the label as we know it today was born. As a nice detail, the wolf comes from the coat of arms of the Lawton family, the former owners. Even today, the vats of Léoville Poyferré are housed in their half of the historic chateau that they share with Léoville Las Cases. More recently, however, the facilities across the road were renovated – and guess which sketch was used as a starting point for the new architecture...

Managing Director Sara Lecompte-Cuvelier

POWERFUL AND LUSH

At Léoville Poyferré, the work in the vineyard is done according to traditional practices: each worker is responsible for his own plots and plants. The terroir of this Second Grand Cru Classé consists of gravel with sand and clay. The vineyards now consist of a total of 80 hectares planted with 65% cabernet sauvignon, 23% merlot, 8% petit verdot and 4% cabernet franc.

All the vineyards are vinified separately in one of the 56 stainless steel tanks before aging for 18 months on oak barrels. The style of Léoville Poyferré is powerful and lush with black fruits. They also make a second wine under the name Pavillon de Léoville Poyferré, which you can also recognise by the label with the light yellow colour and the simple sketch of the current chateau.

MARQUES DE
RISCAL
FINCA TORREA

DOCa Rioja, Spain

THE MARQUIS OF RISCAL

The benchmark of Rioja. You probably recognise the textbook Rioja Reserva by *Herederos del Marqués de Riscal*. It is considered to be the Moët & Chandon Impérial Brut of the DOCa Rioja, Spain's most widely acclaimed wine region. In the past, wine drinkers who wanted to impress friends and family with their bottle of Marqués de Riscal even filled empty bottles with other wine to deceive their ignorant guests.

To prevent counterfeiting, Marqués de Riscal came up with an idea. They started bottling the wine in a bottle with a gold-coloured 'net' that enclosed the neck and cork, making it impossible to uncork the wine without breaking the net. The Rioja Reserva is still bottled that way to this very day. The prestigious 'Diplôme d'Honneur' is shown on the label; Marqués de Riscal won this prize in 1895, the first non-French winemaker to be awarded this honour. From today's perspective, we can agree that the net and the certificate on the label seems fairly old-fashioned. But let's face it, it totally suits the taste of that specific wine.

RIOJA
2.0

'And now for something completely
different', the Marquis must have
thought. What if we stop using the
heavily vanilla-scented American oak
barrels and switch to French barriques?
This would create a totally new style:
fruit-driven, less polished, and
juicier, with excellent drinkability.
Rioja 2.0 is a wine called Finca Torrea,
named after the land (finca) around the
winery in the heart of the complex known
as 'The City of Wine'.

Finca Torrea was launched with the 2006
vintage and quickly became the favourite
Rioja for people who wanted to move beyond
the classic Rioja. This is perfectly
aligned with the pioneering vision of the
Marquis. Let's not forget it was Marqués
de Riscal who personally created the DO
Rueda and introduced fresh, clean and
aromatic verdejo to the world.

Finca Torrea

MAP OF PLOTS

A new wine like Finca Torrea calls for a newly styled label: not rectangular, not round, but an organic shape, just like the plots of the Torrea land. The label shows a top view of the vineyards where the tempranillo and graciano grapes for this wine are grown.

The label is not a stand-alone – just like Marqués de Riscal is not only about Rioja. This means that there is a similar label for a Rueda wine which is also produced by the marquis: the Finca Montico, not your everyday Rueda. This wine has more to offer, since it is made from old vines and 80% of the wine is aged on the lees (dead yeast cells), while the other 20% aged on French oak barrels.

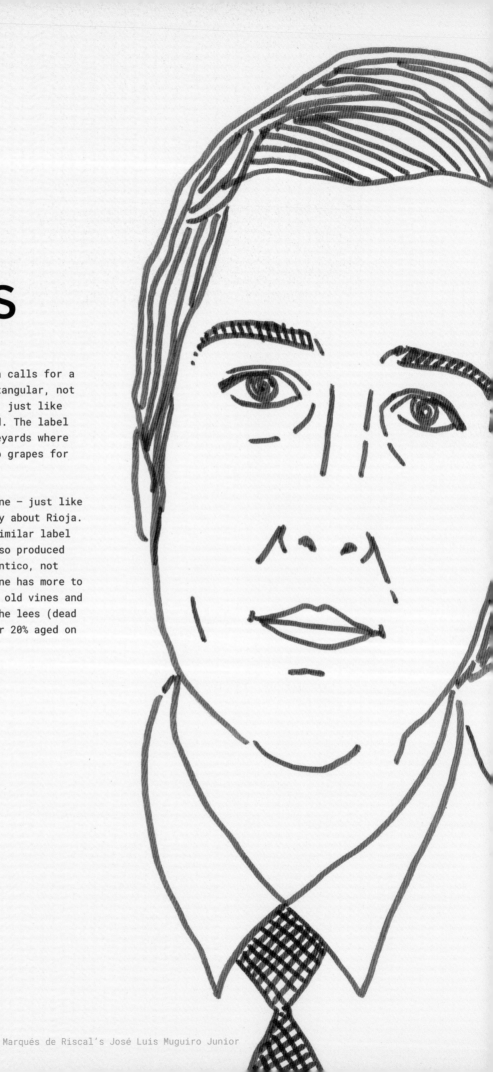

Marqués de Riscal's José Luis Muguiro Junior

THE GUGGENHEIM OF RIOJA

In 1999, world-renowned Canadian architect Frank Gehry designed the Guggenheim Museum in Bilbao. Marqués de Riscal surprised friends and foes when they invited Gehry to design their tasting room. After one glass of Rioja too many, things got out of hand, and Gehry was unstoppable. The result is much, much more than just a simple tasting room.

Nowadays the marquis makes his wines and receives his guests in The City of Wine. The complex includes winemaking and cellar facilities as well as a hotel featuring 43 luxury rooms and suites, as well as a restaurant that holds two Michelin stars, a wellness centre and a *vinothérapie* spa. The design of course is very characteristic of Gehry and has changed the image of Marqués de Riscal from an old-school noble pioneer of wine into a modern producer ready to face the challenges of the 21st century.

CLOUDY
BAY
SAUVIGNON
BLANC

Marlborough, New Zealand

KIWI
SAUVIGNON

There's something about Marlborough. The most famous wine region of New Zealand has this special *je ne sais quoi* that provides the perfect conditions for growing sauvignon blanc. Marlborough is the northernmost wine region of South Island. The region benefits from the cool ocean currents that flow in between the two main islands of New Zealand, where Cook Strait connects the Tasman Sea with the South Pacific Ocean.

Sauvignon blanc originates from the Loire Valley in France. The most famous appellations where this grape is grown are Sancerre and neighbouring Pouilly-Fumé. Of course the French believe that these regions are not only the birthplace of sauvignon blanc, but also the best place to grow it. In terms of climate conditions, Marlborough has proven itself to be at least equally good or even better – but you might want to avoid saying that too loudly when you are in France.

Winemaker Tim Heath and technical director Jim White

AYE CAPTAIN

Cook Strait is named after Captain James Cook, a British seafarer and cartographer. In 1769 Captain Cook was the first European to sail through the strait. On this first voyage of discovery to the Pacific, he sailed around New Zealand. He must have glimpsed Marlborough as he travelled through the strait that was later named after him. So what was his first impression of the region?

Just take a look at the Cloudy Bay label and you'll know: a fog-shrouded, mountainous landscape where the line between water and land is hard to see. This is the key success factor of this wine region today. It does get warm in summer, but the ocean exerts a cooling influence throughout the year. The label is simple and stylish yet elegant. It says it all: 'Cloudy Bay'. Was it a note from Captain Cook's logbook? Or did he name the area Cloudy Bay because of the flooding of the region that coincided with his arrival?

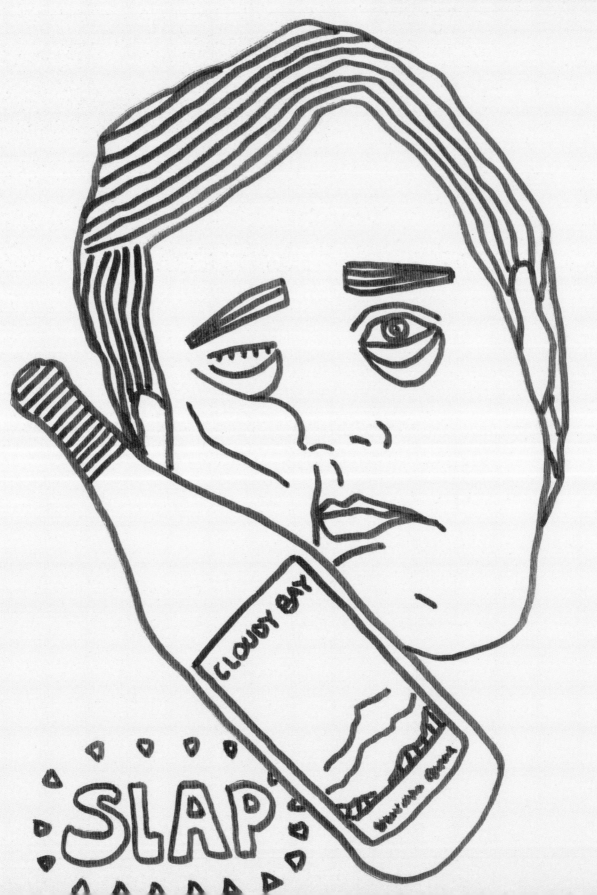

Cloudy Bay Sauvignon Blanc is the benchmark for Marlborough. The wine is made from nine different plots of land. The harvest takes place in cool evening temperatures to retain the freshness in the eventual wine. By far the majority of the blend ferments in stainless steel tanks. Unusually, 5% is fermented in old French oak vats, which gives the final wine more depth and complexity.

If you could give taste a colour, the Cloudy Bay Sauvignon Blanc would be a vibrant, intense green. Close your eyes and think of green asparagus, gooseberry, new-mown grass and freshly chopped green herbs. But there is more: lime, kiwi, Granny Smith. And let's not forget passion fruit. The wine is crisp, tense and mineral: a slap in the face, a wake-up call. Your perfect companion to sushi, Thai crab cakes and Jamaican jerk shrimp.

THE LUXURY BRAND

Cloudy Bay was established in 1985, making it one of the first five producers in the region. Founder David Hohnen, also known from Margaret River's Cape Mentelle (Australia), saw the winemaking potential of Marlborough. The company now has a total of 310 hectares, mainly planted with sauvignon blanc, but also pinot noir and chardonnay.

Cloudy Bay makes an excellent aperitif wine and fits every no-nonsense wine cellar. However, the winery is seen as a luxury brand, and that is due entirely to the umbrella company this brand falls under. The wine is imported to Europe by MHCS, situated on the Avenue de Champagne in Épernay. Together with Cape Mentelle, Cloudy Bay is part of the same portfolio as famous champagne house and luxury brand Veuve Clicquot. Maybe this is the reason why they offer a scenic helicopter tour of the estate that starts from NZ$ 4,500.

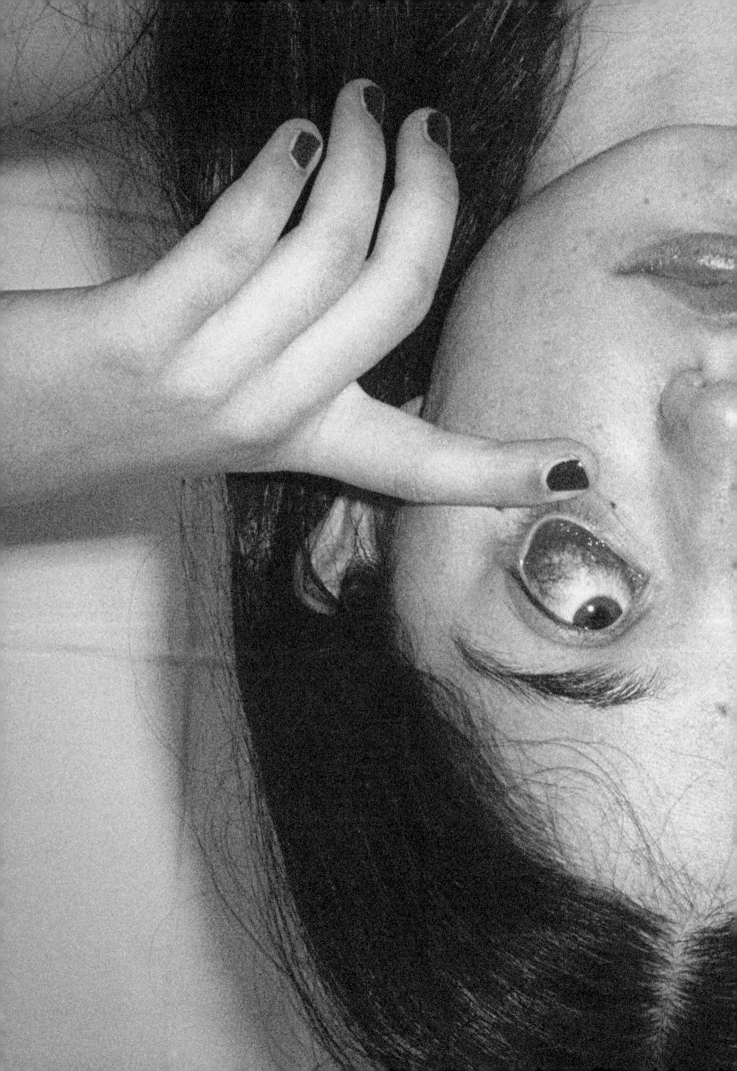

D'ARENBERG
THE
STUMP JUMP
WHITE BLEND

McLaren Vale, Australia

FROM HORSES TO VINES

The drive from Adelaide, the capital city of South Australia, to McLaren Vale only takes 45 minutes. Where Barossa Valley is north from Adelaide, McLaren Vale is south, bordering directly on Gulf St Vincent. This makes the wine region much cooler in temperature than Barossa.

The story of d'Arenberg starts in 1912, when the current owners' great-grandfather sold his horses and started a wine company. Still family-owned, d'Arenberg is currently in the hands of fourth-generation winemaker Chester Osborn. It is considered one of the top producers of the region. They are a proud member of the AFFW: Australia's First Families of Wine, a society of twelve wine families, that all have their own 'landmark wine' in their portfolios.

AN AUSTRALIAN INVENTION

The Stump Jump: not only the name of the wine, it is also a South Australian invention that went all around the world, according to Chester Osborn. This innovative plough made it possible for a ploughshare to jump over tree roots and stumps. It was a huge improvement, since farmers no longer had to stop their horse while ploughing the land. Wondering why you never heard of this fantastic invention before? It may have something to do with the invention of the tractor just a few years later...

The story goes that the inventor of the Stump Jump, Richard Bowyer Smith, had poor eyesight, so it would have been dangerous for him to operate his own machine. To keep a close eye on his deteriorating sight, the inventor had to take regular eye tests. The label of the Stump Jump wines is inspired by Mr Smith, his invention and his handicap.

FROM EYE TEST TO SOBRIETY TEST

The Stump Jump label is based on an eye chart often used by opticians and ophthalmologists. The idea is that the letters on the label get smaller on each line. The official name of this test is a Snellen chart, named after Dutch professor of ophthalmology Herman Snellen, who invented the chart in 1862. Even today, this chart is sold in the US more than any other poster.

The Aussies are an inventive group of people, however, with their own habits and handy ways of discovering unique new approaches. The eye chart has been renamed a sobriety test, and comes with a whole new set of instructions. The official way to do it? Hold the bottle an arm's length away from you and read the smallest letters at the bottom of the label. Can you still read what it says? Then feel free to pour yourself another glass.

Chester Osborn

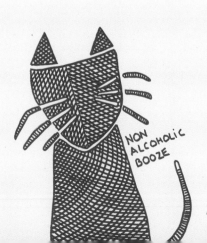

NON ALCOHOLIC BOOZE

As a child Chester had a cat named Non Alcoholic Booze

ONE HUNDRED AND THREE PERCENT GRAPES

The climate of McLaren Vale makes it an ideal location for Rhône grapes. The Stump Jump wines are available in different varieties. Apart from the White Blend, there is a 100% shiraz and a traditional GSM blend of grenache, shiraz and mourvèdre. It doesn't get more Rhône than that. On the other hand, there is a single-variety sauvignon blanc, a riesling and a lightly wooded chardonnay. A Bordeaux blend of cabernet sauvignon and merlot completes the range. All Stump Jump wines over-deliver on fruit-driven and mineral-based drinkability.

The White Blend is a blend made out of riesling, sauvignon blanc and – of course – the Rhône grape varieties marsanne, roussanne and viognier that changes every year. Not all grapes are used in each year's blend. For instance, the 2018 vintage has no viognier in it. According to the d'Arenberg website, that year's wine is 55% riesling, 23% marsanne, 20% sauvignon blanc and 5% roussanne. This unique combination makes The Stump Jump White Blend 2018 the only wine in the world made from 103% grapes. Talking about sobriety tests...

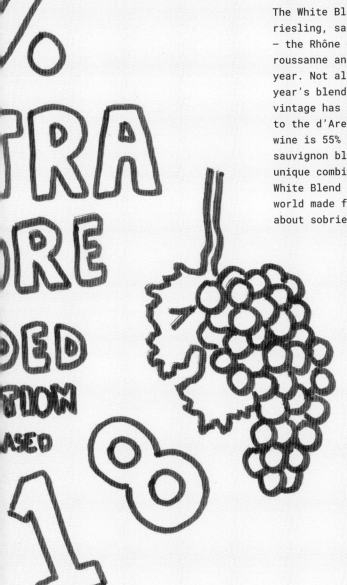

FRANCIS COPPOLA RESERVE CABERNET SAUVIGNON

Sonoma County, USA

TWO GREAT ART FORMS

Francis Ford Coppola is the only winemaker in the world who has won five Academy Awards. He is considered one of the greatest filmmakers of all time. Coppola became world-famous as the director of Apocalypse Now ('I love the smell of napalm in the morning!'), Bram Stoker's Dracula and of course The Godfather Trilogy. But let's not forget that Coppola has been making wine since 1979.

In Coppola's own words, 'Winemaking and filmmaking are two great art forms'. He bought a part of Inglenook Estate that had been making wine for almost a century. He bought back the old vineyards that once belonged to the estate, but also invested in other vineyards in Napa. In 2010 he opened the Francis Ford Coppola Winery in Sonoma County. Another acclaimed director makes his wines these days: Corey Beck is the current 'Director of Winemaking'.

MAKE ME AN OFFER I CAN'T REFUSE

Corey Beck makes wines from Francis Ford Coppola's own vineyards. The flagship wines of the estate are Archimedes and Eleanor, the latter named after Coppola's wife. The wines also include the recognisable Diamond Collection, the Director's Cut and several ranges of entry-level wines that find their way all over the world.

In order to obtain sufficient grapes for all their wines, Coppola has long-term contracts with grape farmers in the region. From that perspective, you can see him as a growers' co-op. Does that mean that Francis Ford Coppola is the Domäne Wachau, La Chablisienne, Mezzacorona or the Martín Códax of the US? He probably prefers to compare himself to Les Grandes Marques from the Champagne region: Moët & Chandon, Veuve Clicquot, Mercier, Gosset, Laurent-Perrier, Billecart-Salmon, Krug, Pol Roger and sixteen other big brands.

Reserve Cabernet Sauvignon.

Francis Coppola

Francis Ford Coppola

FRANCIS' SCRIPTS ARE LIKE A NEWSPAPER

King Cab in optima forma. Bold, rich and direct. Dark, dense and in your face. The 2017 vintage is a single vineyard cabernet sauvignon from Stuhlmuller Vineyard in Alexander Valley, a warm region in the upper Sonoma County, 100 kilometres north of San Francisco. As the Director of Winemaking, Corey Beck gets to hand-select small lots of fruit for the Francis Coppola Reserve range.

The Francis Coppola Reserve Cabernet Sauvignon is only sold to visitors of the winery, 'Wine Family Members' and online shoppers. Buyers can expect a dark-coloured cabernet full of blackberry, black cherry and spices such as cinnamon, dried bay leaf and vanilla. Slightly smoky and oaky with earthy tones and hints of espresso, chocolate and tobacco. Your perfect companion to any type of grilled beef.

Reserve Cabernet Sauvignon

THE COPPOLA TIMES

Apart from the Reserve Cabernet Sauvignon, the total range of Francis Coppola Reserve wines consists of a Chardonnay, Viognier, Pinot Noir, Petite Syrah and Syrah. Five of the wines feature a lady on the label. The Cabernet Sauvignon is the only wine of the range that shows a man, all dressed up in a brown jacket, red tie and yellow shirt completed with a brown hat. The fact that the artist decided to create an artwork featuring a gentleman says it all about the sophisticated character of the cabernet sauvignon grape.

The artist of this label (and all other Francis Coppola Reserve wines) happens to be Dean Tavoularis; his signature is on the label as well. Tavoularis is an art director and production designer who met Francis Ford Coppola during the making of The Godfather. From that movie on, they continued to work together. Tavoularis was responsible for the exterior and interior design of the winery in Sonoma. They collaborated on over a dozen other movies, despite the famous quote by Dean Tavoularis: 'Francis's scripts are like a newspaper. There's a new one every day.'

Francis Coppola

CHATEAU RUBAN
CABERNET
SAUVIGNON
ROSE

Strekov, Slovakia

DANUBE LOWLAND

As the name suggests, Château Rúbaň is situated in the historic village of Rúbaň. The village was first mentioned in 1268, but is now home to only 1,000 inhabitants. Situated in the Strekov region in southern Slovakia, Château Rúbaň is located halfway between the capital cities of Slovakia and Hungary: Bratislava and Budapest. The Danube River flows through both these cities and forms the border between the two countries.

Strekov is part of the Danube Lowland, or *Podunajská nížina*, as they would say in Slovakia. Geomorphologists see the region as a single unit that includes the Austrian Neusiedl Basin and the Hungarian Győr Basin. This wine region gets the most hours of sun in all of Slovakia. Château Rúbaň offers more than wine alone. In addition to their wine tastings, you can spend the night in their guesthouse, organise events on the estate, or even get married in the chateau.

THE USUAL SUSPECTS

At Château Rúbaň, they make wines from
three categories of grape varieties.
In the first place, there are the typical
Danube grapes that you'll also find in
Austria and Hungary: grüner veltliner
(better known locally as veltlínske
zelené), riesling (rizling rýnsky) and
blaufränkisch (frankovka modrá). The
second category consists of the local
varieties: the white svoj sen, noria
and mília. And the black grapes: dunaj
and alibernet. The final category is the
international usual suspects: chardonnay
and cabernet sauvignon.

From the cabernet sauvignon, Château
Rúbaň makes a red wine and a rosé. The
rosé gets its characteristic pink colour
from a few hours of contact with the
grape skins. The colour is slightly
darker than your average Provençal
rosé. The wine is light, fruity, juicy
and inviting. Modern, invigorating and
pure with candied cherries, currant,
blueberries and some lactic hints of
buttermilk and yogurt.

ANIMAL FARM

The label of the Cabernet Sauvignon
Rosé is a single piece showing a woman
herding geese. Four geese walk in front
of her, but if you trace her route, it
leads to another group of four geese
near a number of water plants.

The similarity between Château Rúbaň's
labels is that they excel in their
superb simplicity. Farm animals, people
or modes of transportation feature
prominently on all the labels of Château
Rúbaň. In a couple of cases (such as
the riesling and the dunaj), all these
elements are combined in the same
composition: a horse and carriage and
one or more people in action.

HYBRID GRAPE VARIETIES

There are thousands of different grape varieties. Some grapes are a natural cross between each other. The most famous example of this is cabernet sauvignon, derived from cabernet franc and sauvignon blanc, hence the name cabernet sauvignon.

In addition to natural crossings, there are also hybrid grape varieties that were created by humans. The most successful ones are the South African pinotage (pinot noir x cinsault), the Swiss müller thurgau (riesling x madeleine royal) and the Austrian zweigelt (blaufränkisch x sankt laurent). The 'local' grapes of Château Rúbaň are all hybrids. The aromatic white grape mília is a later generation, crossing müller thurgau and gewürztraminer. Svoj sen is a crossing between three grapes: pinot gris, the Romanian fetească regală and riesling, while noria is a crossing between riesling and sémillon. The black grape dunaj is made from muscat bouschet and blauer portugieser. And as the name alibernet already reveals, it is a hybrid grape made out of cabernet sauvignon and alicante bouschet.

Vladimíra and László, the owners of Château Rúbaň

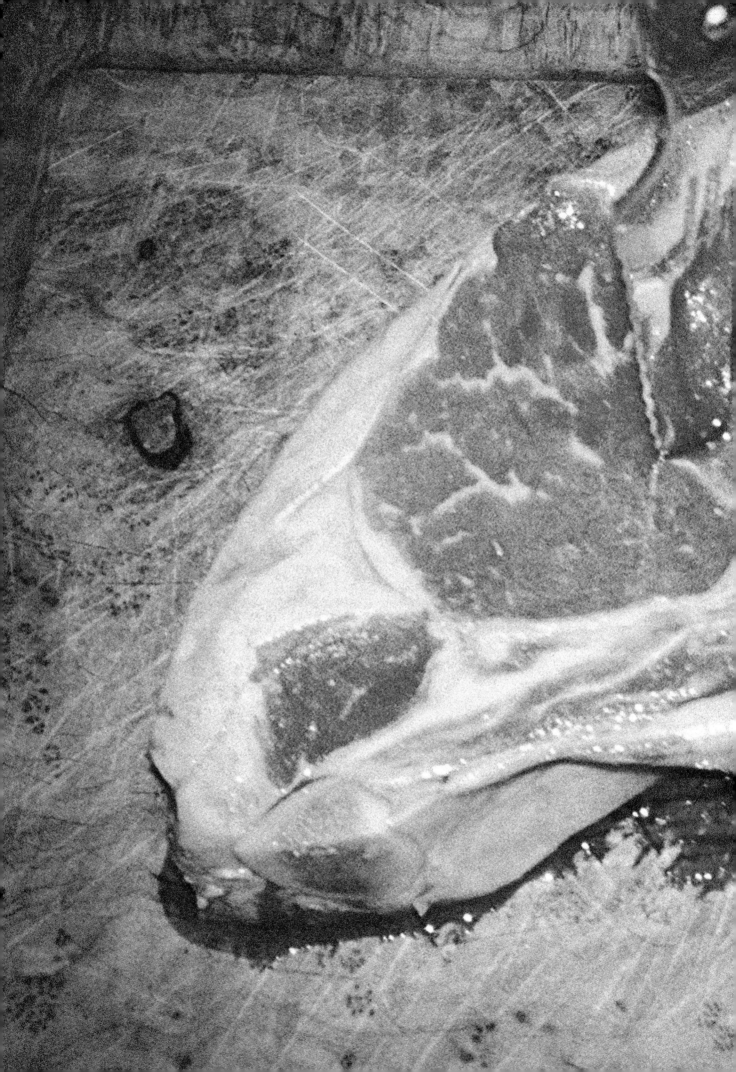

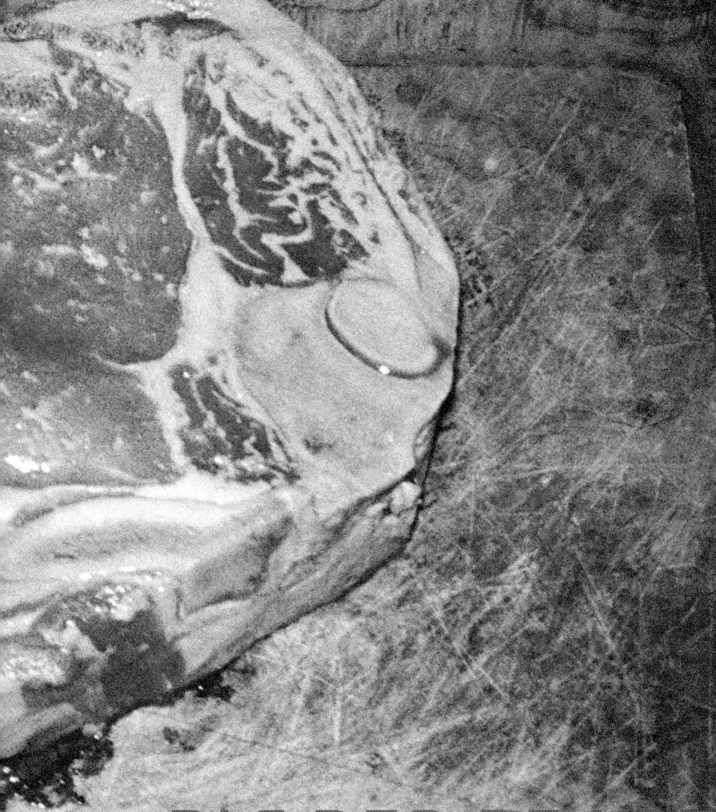

BIG RED BEAST THE WINE LEGEND

Pays d'Oc IGP, France

LET'S TALK ABOUT TANNINS

Any idea why your teeth turn black and your tongue turns purple when drinking red wine? There's a simple answer: tannins. They taste bitter and give an astringent feeling in your mouth. Tannins make you want to drink a glass of water on the side. They come from the grape skin, especially of black grapes, but also from the seeds and stems. In the production of white wines, the grape juice does not come into contact with the skins of the grapes, so there are no tannins in white wine. The exception to the rule is, of course, orange wine...

When working with black grape varieties the eventual level of tannins in the wine is dependent on the characteristics of the grape that has been used and the length of time that the juice is in contact with the skins. Rosé, for example, has extremely brief skin contact and also very low tannins. And in terms of grape varieties pinot noir, gamay and blaufränkisch tend to have low tannins because of their thin skin. In contrast, syrah (shiraz), cabernet sauvignon and malbec are well known for their dark-coloured wines with high tannins.

TANNINS

- STEMS
- SEEDS
- SKINS

PULP FICTION

There is one thing you should know: grape juice is colourless! Not just the juice from white grapes, but black grapes as well. Crazy idea? Not when you think about Blanc de Noirs Champagne: literally white champagne made entirely from pinot noir and or pinot meunier grapes. The exception to the rule is a group of grapes known as 'teinturiers', which are known for their red pulp and automatically produce coloured juice.

A teinturier is often used to make a red wine, and chances are good that your wine will be dark and crimson in colour. Typical examples of a teinturier are dunkelfelder (often found in Germany), saperavi (from the country of Georgia), turán (Hungary) and of course alicante bouschet. This grape was used to give some extra colour to a wine — like a drop of ink. In most cases, this was prohibited by local wine legislation. A wine from alicante bouschet can automatically be called a Big Red Beast.

NOT
AS
BEASTL

So what are your expectations when you see a wine called Big Red Beast with a black label showing a smiling red Yeti carrying two bottles of wine? You would probably think of a 'dark inky red, powerful rich and round, toasted with vanilla aromas'. Your expectations are further nourished by exactly these words on the back label. But to be honest, the Big Red Beast is not as beastly as you might think.

The taste is friendly, featuring blackberry, strawberry and plum, a sweet hint from heavily used oak and an elegant tannin structure. Who would have thought!

ALICANTE FROM LANGUEDOC

The alicante bouschet grapes used for this wine come from the Languedoc in the south of France. Big Red Beast is made by a company called LGI Wines, one of the largest wine companies in France. This Carcassonne-based merchant is a master in creating tailor-made wines or concept brands. Their range also includes a Big White Beast and a Big Pink Beast. Big Red Beast is available in thirteen countries over the world.

The history of Carcassonne goes back to the 8th century BC. The fortified old town, La Cité de Carcassonne, is Europe's largest preserved fortress dating back to the Middle Ages. In Carcassonne, they know that storytelling is just as important as winemaking.

AMON RA

GLAETZER
WINES
AMON-RA

Barossa, Australia

BARON OF THE BAROSSA

The name Glaetzer is iconic within the world of Australian top wines. In just a short time, Ben Glaetzer transformed from Young Winemaker of the Year to become Wine Personality of the Year, New World Winemaker of the Year and even 'Baron of the Barossa'. Who could have imagined this when the Glaetzer family set foot on a steamer heading out from Germany in 1888? It took them seven weeks to trade Brandenburg for Barossa, where they ended up in Nuriootpa. They were among the earliest winemaker families in the Barossa Valley.

It would not be until 1995 that the Glaetzer family would start their own winery. After a successful career creating wines for other producers, it was Collin Glaetzer who founded this boutique winery, with the aim of making super premium Barossa Valley wines. The current driving force behind Glaetzer wines is his son, the widely travelled Ben Glaetzer.

SHIRAZ SPECIALIST

Glaetzer Wines makes four wines, all red and all prominently featuring the shiraz grape. The flagship wine, Amon-Ra, is made of 100% shiraz. Another 100% shiraz, Bishop bears the maiden name of Ben's mother, Judith. Then there is Anaperenna, a blend of shiraz with cabernet sauvignon referencing the Roman goddess of the new year. Finally, Wallace is a blend of shiraz with grenache, and was named after an ancestral family line from Scotland, tracing back from Ben's mother.

Amon-Ra is an amazing wine, a beast, a powerhouse. As dark as ink, tough, solid, full and rich. Yet the wine has enough smoothness on the palate, which is quite exceptional for a wine with 15.5% alcohol. The taste is as deep and rich as its colour, with blackberry, blackcurrant and black cherry. There is also vanilla, cedar wood, cigar box, tobacco and a rich scent of saddle leather. The wine has a high viscosity, with peaty whisky-like tones, as if the neighbour were lighting up the barbecue. In terms of drinkability, Amon-Ra is simply extraordinary.

THE EYE OF HORUS

The name Amon-Ra comes from ancient Egypt: in Egyptian mythology, Amon was a primordial god and Ra was the sun god. Ra is often depicted with the body of a human and the head of a falcon. In later myths, the two fused into one supreme god. Amon-Ra is the flagship of Glaetzer Wines, which easily explains the comparison with the supreme ruler of ancient Egyptian divinity.

All the Glaetzer wines have a black and white label with a symbol that characterises the wine. In the case of Amon-Ra it shows the Eye of Horus, or wedjat, the ancient Egyptian symbol of protection, power and good health. Amon-Ra was created to appeal to six senses. You can *see*, *smell* and *taste* the wine, while the mouthfeel incorporates your sense of *touch*. *Listen* to how it speaks to you — and *think* about the experience for a long, lingering time.

SIX SENSES

Amon-Ra

WINE GROWING HISTORY

Winemaking in Egypt dates back to 3000 BC, and has played a major role in the development of wine as we know it today. The temple of Amon-Ra is believed to be the first in the world to plant a monoculture vineyard for the production of wine. While the ancient Egyptians made wine as part of a ceremonial practice, it was the ancient Greeks who began producing wine for general consumption. The Romans made wine mainstream as a safe drink for soldiers, preventing food poisoning from unsafe water, and the Catholic Church spread viticulture to the New World as part of its Holy Mass rituals.

So can Egypt boast the world's oldest wine cultivation? No. Archaeological finds show that the wine culture in today's Georgia and Armenia dates back to at least 8,000 years ago, making these countries the cradle of wine-growing.

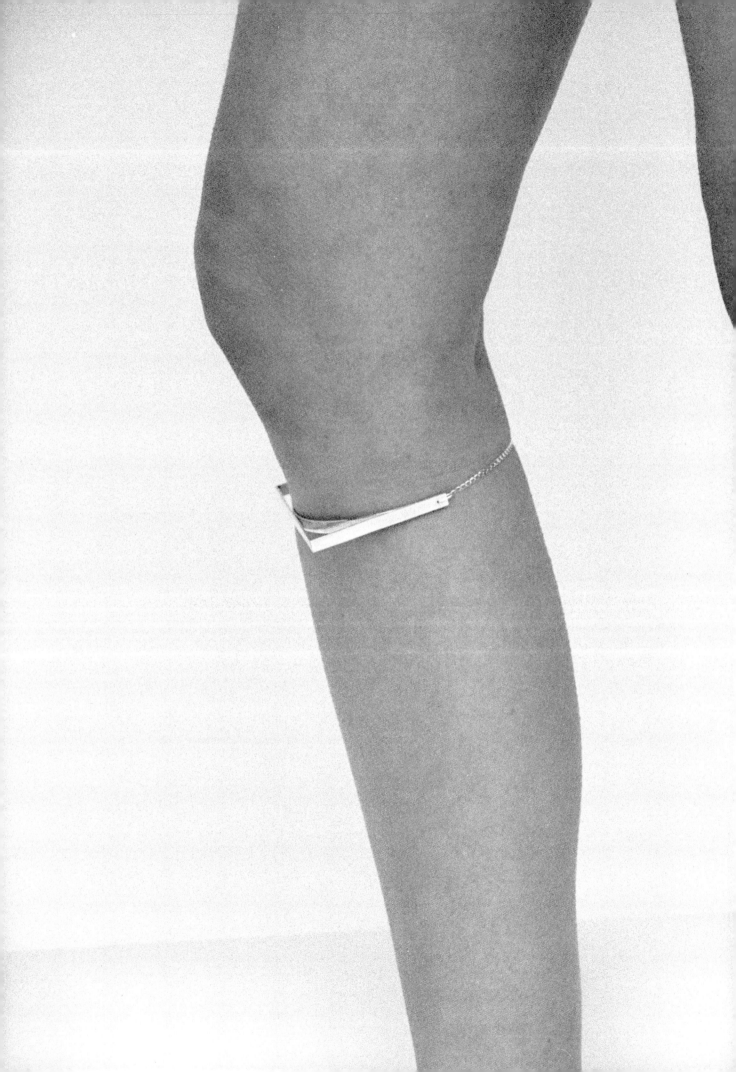

WEINGUT KLAUS ZIMMERLING SUPER NATURAL SPATBURGUNDER

Sachsen, Germany

FOUNTAIN FIGURES

What you see on the label of this sparkling wine is a sculpture created by Polish-born artist Małgorzata Chodakowska, who has lived in Germany since 1991. She is well known for her qualities as a sculptor and loves to work with wood and bronze; her 'fountain figures' incorporate sculptures with water features. In the piece depicted here, the fountain flows from the woman's hair.

Małgorzata Chodakowska and Klaus Zimmerling

Chodakowska is known for creating images of strong women and playful children. Her most famous statue is in Dresden's Heidefriedhof cemetery. Titled *Trauerndes Mädchen am Tränenmeer* (Mourning girl by the sea of tears), it commemorates the citizens of Dresden who died during the bombardment of 13, 14 and 15 February 1945. Much of her work has been installed on the wine estate operated by her husband, Klaus Zimmerling, and one of her artworks is used for the label of the wines produced by Weingut Klaus Zimmerling every year.

August II the Strong, King of Poland and Elector of Saxony

THE ROYAL VINEYARD

At Weingut Klaus Zimmerling, it is all about quality rather than quantity. The estate is situated in Pillnitz, on the banks of the river Elbe in the Sachsen wine region, around the city of Dresden. Weingut Klaus Zimmerling has only four hectares, but produces a wide range of different grape varieties, including riesling, grauburgunder, weissburgunder, kerner, gewürztraminer and traminer.

Klaus Zimmerling and Małgorzata Chodakowska have lived here since 1992 and work their vines on the Pillnitzer Königlicher Weinberg: the royal vineyard of Pillnitz, which was named after its former owner, August II the Strong, King of Poland and Elector of Saxony. Considering the vineyard's history, it is a striking detail is that the estate is now in the hands of a German-Polish couple.

Super Natural · Zero Dosage Spätburgunder

Weingut Klaus Zimmerling

NO
SKIN
CONTACT

Saxony, or Sachsen as the locals call it, is a region that is better known for its white grape varieties. This sparkling wine, however, is made from the spätburgunder, a black grape variety. Due to the lack of skin contact, the wine is white.

After more than five years of ripening, with most of that time spent in the bottle, the colour of this sparkling white wine is slowly darkening as it ages. The wine's scent is very mature, rich and ripe. The overall character is dark and full-bodied, yet the wine contains a beautiful acidity, crisp and crystal clear with notes of grapefruit, currant, cherries and strawberry. At the same time, some apple can be detected, with hints of spices and tobacco and earthy tones of forest floor and autumn leaves.

CHAMPAGNE VS SPARKLING WINE

Over the centuries, champagne has become such a world-famous name that it is almost synonymous with sparkling wine. So can we call this wine champagne? No, of course not; only sparkling wines that come from the Champagne region in France can be given that protected title. This wine is made from spätburgunder, exactly the same grape variety as pinot noir. The vinification technique is also identical to champagne, involving a second fermentation inside the bottle. The name Zero Dosage is also used for champagne and means that there is no added sugar in the wine. Despite all that, we still have to call this a sparkling wine – or as the Germans would say, a Sekt.

A sparkling wine made exclusively from black grapes is called a Blanc de Noirs: white wine from black grapes. In the champagne region, a Blanc de Noir is a white champagne made from either pinot noir or pinot meunier, or a blend of these two grape varieties. When we refer to Blanc de Blancs champagne, the wine is made from white grapes only, and in almost all cases 100% chardonnay.

DOMAINE
SANGOUARD-
GUYOT
MÂCON-
VERGISSON
LAROCHE

AOP Mâcon-Vergisson, France

WHEN
TWO
BECOME
ONE

Pierre-Emmanuel Sangouard and Catherine Guyot both come from a family of winemakers with a history dating back to the 19th century. When they got married, the domains of two families became one: Domaine Sangouard-Guyot. Since that day, they jointly own 12 hectares in the Mâconnais. Their vineyards are divided across 34 individual plots, all planted with a single grape: chardonnay.

At Domaine Sangouard-Guyot, they make eight wines a year, including four different Pouilly-Fuissé wines, which is considered the top appellation for Mâconnais. They also produce wines in the neighbouring appellations of Saint-Véran, Mâcon-Villages, Mâcon-Bussières, and the location of the featured wine: Mâcon-Vergisson. The vineyards of Domaine Sangouard-Guyot are located between the iconic landmarks of La Roche de Solutré and La Roche de Vergisson.

ROCK
'N'
ROLL

These two enormous limestone landmarks at Vergisson and Solutré were formed from fossilised coral plateaus 160 million years ago, when this entire region was a sea. It's the perfect explanation for the surrounding vineyard soils, rich in marine fossils and limestone. Many fossilised bones were found near La Roche de Solutré, including reindeer, wolves, mammoths and even sabre-toothed tigers. Take a look at the shape of the escarpment and it's clear that prehistoric man probably literally chased their prey over the cliff.

La Roche de Solutré is the iconic Eiffel Tower of the Mâconnais. The rock features prominently on every label of Domaine Sangouard-Guyot, accompanied by the limestone protrusion of La Roche de Vergisson. The label consists of a single piece and contains all the information you need to know as a wine lover: producer, origin, vintage, alcohol percentage and contents. There is only one thing you won't find on the label: which grape variety has been used.

Mâcon-Vergisson La Roche

Domaine Sangouard-Guyot

LITTLE BROTHER

Of course this wine is made from 100% chardonnay; it's so self-evident that they don't even bother to mention it on the label. Why should they? The Mâconnais is one vast ocean of chardonnay. The grapes for the Mâcon-Vergisson 'La Roche' come from a plot of 0.5 hectares that produce only 3,300 bottles a year. The grapes are grown on the slopes of La Roche de Vergisson, which is why its name is appended to this wine, which is considered Pouilly-Fuissé's 'little brother'.

The wine ages ten months on oak barrels. The result is rich and buttery, yet elegant, vivid and juicy with wild peach, lemon curd, vanilla beans and an herbal note: a textbook Mâconnais.

LAND OF THE FREE

The Mâconnais is the southernmost point of Burgundy and its wines offer great value for money. One of the reasons for this affordability is the lack of vineyards with Premier Cru status. In 1940, the Nazis occupied the northern part of France, including all the northern subregions of Burgundy. The Mâconnais was the only region that remained free. Under Nazi rule, the occupying forces were permitted to send the very best Burgundy wines (Grand Cru) off to Germany, while the troops were allowed to drink the basic wines.

So the French came up with a plan to save as many of their wines as possible. Their solution was a new classification named Premier Cru, produced by the second-best vineyards and made for the French only. It was in their own best interests to designate as many vineyards as possible as Premier Cru, and they did so to the best of their ability. In the Mâconnais, however, there was no need for such a distinction, since all their wines were for the French anyway. After the country's liberation, the French had better things to do than to change their system all over again. Accordingly, the northern part of Burgundy kept their Premier Cru vineyards, and the Mâconnais still has none. However, they have been trying to obtain Premier Cru status for their best 'climats' for several decades.

Domaine Sangouard-Guyot

BOEKEN-
HOUTSKLOOF
SYRAH

Swartland, South-Africa

RAVINE OF THE CAPE BEECH

Boekenhoutskloof (pronounce: *book-en-howds-klohf*) is a South African estate based in Franschhoek. The farm was established in 1776, but has been in the hands of the current owners since 1993. Their first vintage, back in 1996, consisted of only 6,000 bottles, but they have grown significantly since then. They produce millions of litres a year now, not only under the Boekenhoutskloof name, but also under their other brands, which include entry-level Porcupine Ridge, over-performer The Wolftrap, and new kid on the block Cap Maritime. Their famous brand The Chocolate Block is the most successful premium blend of South Africa.

The estate's name translates as 'ravine of the Cape beech tree', an indigenous evergreen tree that grows wild in South Africa and was often used to make furniture in the 18th and 19th century. That connection is why there are still seven chairs on the label of the Boekenhoutskloof wines.

NO TWO LABELS ARE THE SAME

The line-up of chairs on the label includes a country-style split splat chair, a Cape Sandveld chair and a transitional Tulbagh chair. The chairs are a reminder of the 18th century craftsmanship that went into making such beautiful furniture. They provide a powerful metaphor for the craftsmanship of the winemaker in making the best possible wine. It's about creating beauty from natural sources, crafting until you achieve the desired result.

All Boekenhoutskloof labels are torn by hand, ensuring that no two labels are the same. The printing company handles the actual tearing of the labels, while the Boekenhoutskloof staff applies all labels by hand. In total, this provides full-time employment for seven people. In the words of managing partner and technical director Marc Kent, this practice is 'f*cking expensive, but it looks great'. It totally suits his motto for winemaking: 'We're never gonna get rich, but we're gonna have a lot of fun staying poor'.

Marc Kent

Syrah

Boekenhoutskloof

SWARTLAND GRAPES

The four Boekenhoutskloof wines are the white *Semillon* and a trio of reds: the bold, heavy *Stellenbosch Cabernet Sauvignon*, the far more elegant *Franschhoek Cabernet Sauvignon* and the Syrah. The grapes for the syrah are sourced from two company-owned properties in Swartland: Goldmine and Porseleinberg.

Boekenhoutskloof has special ties to Rhône grapes in general and syrah in particular. The Chocolate Block is also syrah-dominated, and all The Wolftrap wines are made from almost only Rhône varieties. Over the years, the Boekenhoutskloof Syrah has always matured on used large oak. The 2018 vintage matured for 18 months on 2,500-litre foudres and 600-litre demi-muids. The result is rich, generous, juicy and fruity with an extremely high drinkability.

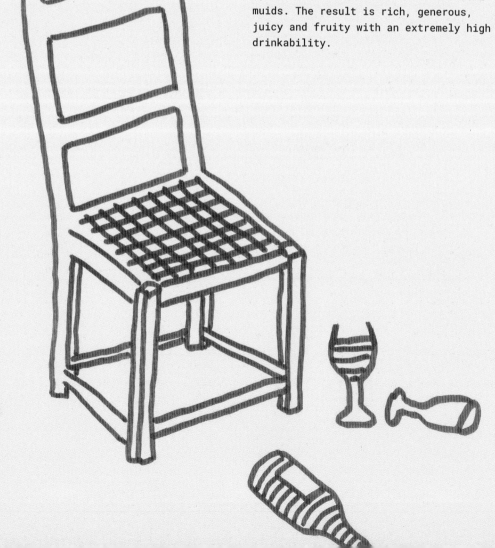

OO = OE + EN   -S   R = skl

A WINE THAT HAS NEVER BEEN SOLD

Besides its home base in Franschhoek, Boekenhoutskloof owns properties in Stellenbosch and Swartland, with a more recent acquisition in the Upper Hemel-en-Aarde Valley. One of the reasons for this is the success of The Chocolate Block, a stand-alone brand which is increasing in popularity. As the managing partner explains, the winery quickly realised they needed to own vineyards.

The new properties enable Boekenhoutskloof to come up with new high-end wines. One of them is Porseleinberg: a single estate, single block 100% syrah from the property in Swartland that shares the same name as the wine. If you think this $100 wine is the absolute pinnacle of the Boekenhoutskloof wines, then you probably haven't heard of The Journeyman yet. This blend of cabernet franc and merlot from the Franschhoek estate is only produced in exceptional vintages. The grape juice finds its way from the vine to the bottle without any pumps. No one actually knows what a bottle of The Journeyman would cost, since it has never been sold – only gifted to the happy few.

GRAVNER
RIBOLLA

Venezia Giulia IGT, Italy

THE RED MOUNTAIN

"Thanks for your interest, but we are not participating in such initiatives." The response received from Gravner was to be expected. At Gravner, everything is about one thing and one thing only: making wine. All decisions made in the vineyard and in the cellar are based on the position of the moon. This is biodynamics to the max. Welcome to the exact border between Italy and Slovenia.

Friuli vineyards are known for the fact that they continue across the Slovenian border – which is quite logical, considering the fact that people were making wine here ages before the border was made. In actual fact, Gravner has vineyards both in Italy and in Slovenia. During World War I, the land of his ancestors became a battlefield where the Italian front faced off against the Austro-Hungarian forces. During that period, the Gravner family residence was used as a Red Cross first aid post even as Monte Sabotino was drenched in the blood of the soldiers who fell there. 90,000 casualties were counted in total, and 29,000 soldiers died at the Battle of Gorizia.

NOIR DE BLANCS

Joško Gravner is the man who believed in orange wine before millennials had reached legal drinking age. Together with his neighbour, Stanko Radikon, he is responsible for the reintroduction of this 'new kid on the block' — but orange wine is as ancient as can be. The traditional production method is still used in the country of Georgia, a region where wines have been made for over 8,000 years. In this former Soviet republic, they are called *qvevri* wines, named after the clay vessels the grapes are fermented in.

Orange wines are skin-fermented amber-coloured wines made from white grapes; it would not be inaccurate to call them *Noir de Blancs*. Fermentation at Gravner takes places in Georgian amphorae buried under the ground. The wine is fermented using natural yeasts that occur on the grape skins. The skins and seeds of the grapes stay in contact with the wine, providing not only its distinctive colour, but also a very specific taste of sage, bark, nuts, juniper, beeswax and an extraordinary mouthfeel rich in tannins.

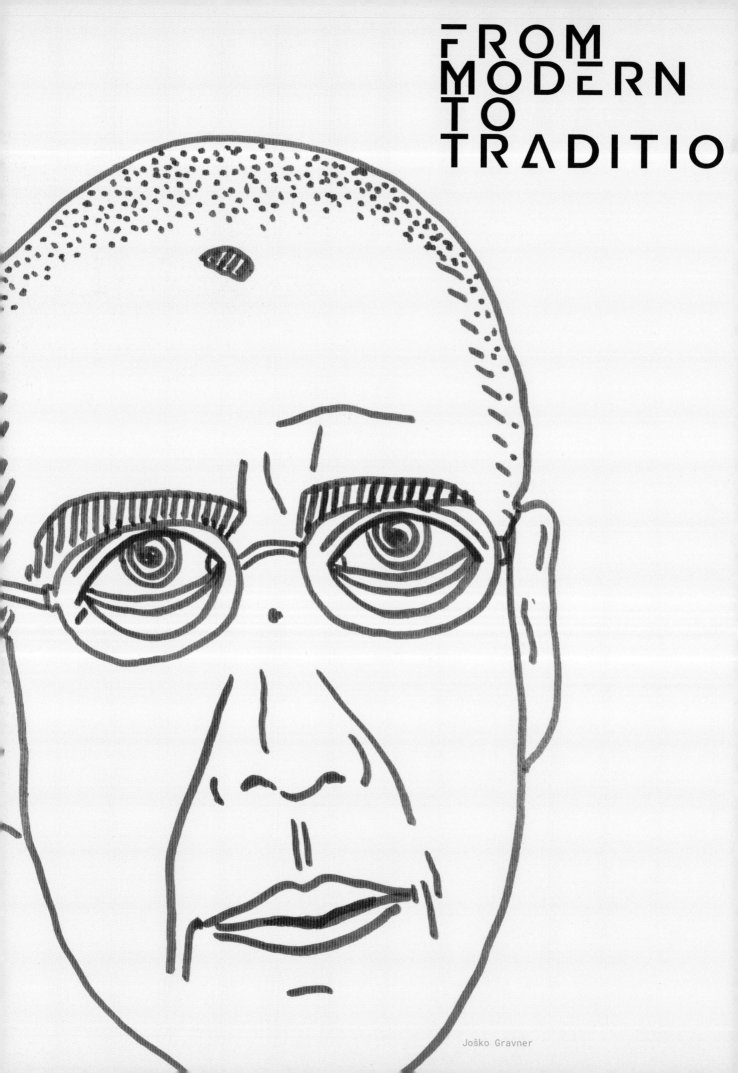

FROM
MODERN
TO
TRADITIO

Joško Gravner

In his younger years, Joško Gravner was reluctant to copy the winemaking methods of his father and uncle. When he became head of the company in the early 1980s, he decided to implement new approaches that he had picked up during his studies. Joško experimented with modern techniques and devices, including stainless steel tanks and aging on barriques. It took him many vintages, a harvest-destroying hailstorm in 1996, and a trip to the Georgian wine region of Kakheti to come to the same conclusion as his father and uncle: let's make wine the way people have been doing for thousands of years.

Back to basics was Gravner's new direction, a transition that took him over a decade. These days, it takes him seven years to release a wine. Contemplate that in terms of return on investment...

BORDERS BECOME BOUNDLESS

Gravner added ponds in his vineyards to enrich the natural ecosystem. The local birds and insects all serve their purpose and have their own impact on the eventual wine — but don't expect to see any of that featured on his bottles. The labels are dark, crimson, minimalistic and down-to-earth. Just like his approach to wine-making, it symbolises his boundlessness.

The old grapevine on his label might have been planted in 1919, right after the war in which thousands of young men died fighting over a border. It is quite ironic to realise that Joško Gravner is a Slovenian man living on the Italian side of the border, making wine in both countries which is sought after around the world.

Istria, Croatia

THE FIVE ASPECTS OF TERROIR

Much has been said and written about terroir. Some say the term refers to the soil of the vineyard, but it goes beyond that. Terroir is a mixture of five different elements, which combine uniquely to ensure that every wine in the world tastes different. The terroir elements are the *grape*, the *climate*, the *soil*, the *sun exposure* of the vineyard and the influences of the *winemaker*.

At Piquentum they strongly believe that at least three of these five elements are the same every year: grape, soil and exposure. This means that the annual variation in flavour depends on human factors and climate conditions. The winemaker decides the moment of harvest, but the amount of rainfall throughout the year determines the final differences in the taste of the vintage and quality of the wine. This fact is the starting point for the new labels of the Piquentum wines.

ADC EUROBEST AND CANNES LION

Some wines are awarded many medals –
but in this case, the wine's label has
won several awards. In this case, we're
not looking at Parker points, Decanter
World Wine Awards or the International
Wine & Spirits Competition. Instead,
the prizes for this label are an ADC
Gold Cube, Eurobest Silver and a Bronze
Lion (Cannes). Titled 'Art directed by
nature', the campaign was developed by
the Croatian advertising agency Studio
Sonda in collaboration with the local
meteorological institute.

The design of the label is fully focused
on providing information to the consumer
about the climate conditions in effect
for this particular vintage of the wine.
To be more precise, the label is a
schematic representation of the monthly
rainfall in the vineyard. You see 12
circles representing the full harvest
year. From left to right and from top to
bottom, the circles represent the months
of October to September. The larger the
circle, the more precipitation fell in
that month.

FROM FRANCE TO ISTRIA

Located in the Croatian town of Buzet, Piquentum is an Istrian wine company owned by Dimitri Brečević. He had a French mother and an Istrian father, and was born in the Jurançon region of France. From there, Brečević worked his way around from Domaine de Chevalier (Grand Cru Classé de Graves, Pessac-Léognan) to various estates in Burgundy, eventually moving on to Australia and New Zealand. In 2004 he decided to manage his own estate in his father's homeland: Istria.

Piquentum is the ancient Roman name for the hilltop in Buzet. Brečević currently owns 4.5 hectares of vineyards planted with several local grape varieties: malvazija (white), teran and refošk (black). In his wines, he tries to express the characteristics of Istria.

TERAN AND REFOSK

The name Crno Vino Vrh literally means 'top-quality red wine'. It is made of a grape called teran. This is the local name for terrano, also known as refosco d'Istria or refosco terrano. The distinctions are quite confusing, since the other red wine produced by Piquentum is made from refošk. To complicate matters even more, the two grapes are considered the same variety in Slovenia, but change in name depending on the soil the grapes are planted on.

While refošk often has high alcohol and low acidity, teran offers exactly the opposite: low alcohol and high acidity. The Crno Vino Vrh is light and aromatic. In terms of flavour, it could be compared to gamay and pinot noir, but with a more pronounced acidity. It tastes of pomegranate, raspberry, red currant and some lactic notes. Crno Vino Vrh is the perfect wine to drink slightly chilled with some Istrski pršut (a local prosciutto) while sitting outside and watching the sunset.

WEINGUT AUGUST KESSELER THE DAILY AUGUST PINOT NOIR

Rheingau, Germany

THE POWER OF CHANGE

The year was 1977 when August Kesseler became managing director — or 'Geschäftsführer' as they would say in Germany — at the tender age of nineteen. His parents' company only covered a modest 2.5 hectares at that time, the equivalent of five football pitches. Until that time, August's parents had sold their wines made from riesling or pinot noir by the barrel. From the outset, August felt that he had the power to change the way things worked at Weingut August Kesseler.

He bottled the first wines on the estate in 1979. Step by step, August bought up extra plots containing the best vineyards of the Rheingau. By now, Weingut August Kesseler owns a total of 33 hectares situated exclusively in Erste Lagen and Grosse Lagen. These vineyards can easily be compared with their French counterparts: Premier Cru and Grand Cru. One thing never changed from the moment that August Kesseler took over the Weingut, however. Regardless of how much they expanded, it was still all about the two flagship grapes of Germany, the Rheingau in general and the estate in particular: riesling and pinot noir.

August Kesseler

THE DIVA OF THE VINEYARD

There is something about pinot noir, the grape known in Germany as spätburgunder. As August Kesseler puts it, all of his wines made from pinot noir have "a delicate, feminine, almost erotic character. They flow like cool silk over tender skin." Let those words echo in your ears the next time you sip your pinot noir.

The grape originates from Burgundy and is known for its thin, light-coloured skin. As a result, pinot noir can only be planted in cooler climates. Winemakers consider pinot noir as demanding, in terms of both cultivation and wine production. The diva of the vineyard needs special attention, devotion and care – not least because of its exceptionally long growing season. The German word spät literally means 'late', referring to how late in the season this grape is fully ripe and ready to be picked.

August Kesseler makes a total of
seventeen different wines varying in
grape, origin, quality and vinification
method. This includes a Blanc de Noirs
and a noble sweet Riesling Spätlese.
The entry-level wines of August Kesseler
are called The Daily August, and are
available in white, red and rosé.

The Daily August Pinot Noir is all about
finesse. Like all the pinot noirs by
August Kesseler, the wine ages on oak
barrels, but never more than 30% new.
The charming fruit of the grape always
remains the key success factor of the
wine. The grapes come from steeply
sloping vineyards in Lorch, Rüdesheim
and Assmannshausen. The wine is bursting
with flavours of raspberry, black cherry,
cassis and red pepper.

THE GOOD NEWS

The concept behind The Daily August is
based on a collaboration between the
winemakers of Weingut August Kesseler and
sommeliers from top restaurants. The idea
was to come up with a wine that can be
served by the glass, but still needed to
meet the standards of extremely demanding
guests. Or as Kesseler himself says, "a
wine that is as natural to everyday life
as leafing through a newspaper". The only
difference is that a glass of The Daily
August guarantees instant enjoyment.

Designed in red, white and black, the
label of The Daily August Pinot Noir is
basic but stylish, precise and direct —
just like the taste of the wine. On its
own, it may seem simple, but wait until
you see it in context with the rest of
the wines from the estate. All together,
they create an impressive and colourful
line-up.

POL ROGER
BRUT
RESERVE

AOC Champagne, France

THE MOST BRITISH OF ALL

What do Pol Roger, Johnnie Walker and Angostura Bitters have in common? They are all Royal Warrant holders. Their bottles carry a Royal Warrant reading: 'By Appointment to HM The Queen'. And even though the house is based in champagne capital Épernay, Pol Roger is considered the most British of all champagnes.

Pol Roger himself was only 18 years of age when he founded his own champagne house in 1849. He started out in his small yet famous village of Aÿ, but within two years he moved to the epicentre of the Champagne region: Épernay, where the house is still based. You can find the visitors' centre on the Avenue de Champagne, but the headquarters are on the Rue Winston Churchill, named after the man who more than once called Pol Roger 'the world's most drinkable address'.

PURE
BRIGHT
AND
CLEAN

The white label of the Pol Roger Brut
Réserve is straightforward, basic and
minimalistic. At the same time, however,
it perfectly reflects the brand values
of Pol Roger: pure, bright and clean,
both in terms of business and in taste.
What you see is what you get from this
family-owned champagne brand.

Besides the Brut Réserve, which gives an
excellent first impression of the house
style, Pol Roger produces another six
wines: Pure Extra Brut, Rich Demi Sec,
Brut Vintage, Blanc de Blancs Vintage and
Rosé Vintage. Their Cuvée de Prestige,
called 'Sir Winston Churchill', was first
released in 1984. The cuvée is always
a vintage made from pinot noir with
chardonnay from Grand Cru vineyards that
are owned by Pol Roger. Cuvée Sir Winston
Churchill ('my tastes are simple; I am
easily satisfied with the best') is still
only made in the best vintages. Its very
first vintage was made from grapes from
the year 1975, exactly ten years after
Churchill's death.

Brut Réserve

Pol Roger

THE ROYAL BRUT

The Pol Roger Brut Réserve is made from equal parts of pinot noir, pinot meunier and chardonnay from 30 different crus. The blend consists of 25% reserve wines from other vintages. This makes it possible to come up with a taste-consistent identity that can be best described as elegance with style and quality. The style combines complexity, balance and distinction. It is powerful and vivid with pear, mango, honey, jasmine and vanilla, rich in flavours of apricot jam, orange zest, cardamom and anise.

The Brut Réserve was served in 2011 at the royal wedding of Prince William and Kate Middleton. In 2018, it featured prominently on the wine list at the reception of the royal wedding between Meghan Markle and Prince Harry. Wondering which canapés are best to serve with Pol Roger Brut Réserve? According to Meghan and Harry, the best options are 'Scottish langoustines wrapped in smoked salmon with citrus crème fraîche', 'garden pea panna cotta with quail eggs and lemon verbena' and 'croquette of confit Windsor lamb, roasted vegetables and shallot jam'.

A MUTUAL LOVE

The love between Winston Churchill and Pol Roger came from both sides. Churchill was a generous customer, and a very loyal one: he also called his racehorse Pol Roger after his favourite champagne brand.

Normally, champagne houses are dying to get a role in a Hollywood production. The best example is Bollinger, the favourite champagne of a very high-profile cinematic character: James Bond. During production of the movie Darkest Hour, about Churchill and his role in World War II, the production team approached Pol Roger instead of the other way around, requesting several bottles of the famous Vintage 1928 to appear on screen. Unfortunately, Churchill himself had already consumed the total production from that year. To accommodate the studio, Pol Roger created dummy bottles of the 1928 Vintage and filled them with Brut Réserve.

CLOS SAINT
FIACRE
ORLÉANS
ROUGE

Orléans AOC, France

THE COMPLEXITY OF SIMPLICITY

What do we see here? A man; a French farmer, as we can see by what he's wearing on his head. And he likes wine, simply because he's holding a bottle in his one hand and a glass in the other. He specifically likes this wine, as we can tell by the heart on the glass. And that's it! Nothing more, nothing less. The label comes from Dutch designer Max Kisman, who specialises in the complexity of simplicity: "A beautiful wine deserves a great label."

Amsterdam-based wine importer David Bolomey immediately fell in love with this lip-smacking red on a terrace in Paris. He visited Hubert Piel and decided to bring his wines to the Netherlands. Just one problem: the producer had recently changed the label design, and Bolomey was not a fan. And so Bolomey suggested making a new one, just for the Dutch market. He asked Kisman for the design, and they were all set. Or were they?

Hubert Piel and Bénédicte Montigny-Piel

UNOFFICIAL VIN NATURE

Once Bolomey's personal label was on the wine, he felt that he could also request some extra perks. To cater to the tastes of his clientele and his own personal preferences, he asked winemaker Hubert Piel to make this wine as natural as possible: unfiltered and minimal added sulphites in the end product. Initially a bit reluctant, Hubert later changed his mind, resulting in this 'unofficial vin nature'.

Most of the wines produced in the Orléans appellation come from the local cooperative and find their way to the nearby Parisian bistros. Clos Saint-Fiacre makes their own wine and is in the hands of Bénédicte and Hubert Montigny-Piel. Although they farm their 20 hectares according to organic principles, they are (deliberately) not certified organic. Since changing their recipe for the Dutch wines, they monitored the results with extra care and attention – and liked the new method so much better that they no longer filter any of their own wines either.

Dutch designer Max Kisman

Orléans Rouge

Clos Saint Fiacre

Orléans is not only the most northern subregion of the Loire valley; it is also the closest to Paris. This strategic location is exactly why these vineyards are here… and also why their wines are relatively unknown worldwide, and completely inaccessible. Simply put: they drink it all in Paris, just like Milan drinks up the harvest of Franciacorta. In the Orléans AOC, white wines are made from chardonnay (although pinot gris is also allowed) and rosé and red wines are made from pinot meunier and pinot noir.

The Clos Saint Fiacre Orléans Rouge is made from 100% pinot meunier. The key success factor of the wine is that it was not crafted for sipping, but is a nice drinking wine. Fresh and light with a high acidity, it is the perfect wine to drink slightly chilled on the banks of the Seine on a warm day. Full of red fruits, its flavour is rich in raspberry, strawberry, red cherry, currant, cranberry and pomegranate, with light tannins. A distant association with such cheeses as Brie and Camembert can be attributed to the natural touch. It is an intelligent wine, and very inviting.

CHAMPAGNE GRAPES

Pinot meunier is a famous black grape, but rarely encountered on its own as a red wine. If you've ever had a glass of champagne, you've probably had meunier before. It is the number-three grape in the region, after pinot noir and chardonnay. Interestingly, all three are also used in Orléans.

Most champagne houses use pinot meunier in their blend. Even though meunier (and pinot noir) are black grapes, their juice is colourless, so their champagne is white. The regular Moët & Chandon Impérial Brut, for instance, is 30-40% pinot meunier. The prestige cuvée Dom Pérignon and many other top champagnes are made with only pinot noir and chardonnay. On the other hand, the latest edition of the Krug Grande Cuvée has 22% meunier in its final composition. According to Krug, the taste is in the terroir and not only in the grape. Pinot meunier is perfectly capable of bringing the taste of the terroir into the final wine – not only in champagne, but also in Orléans.

Orléans Rouge

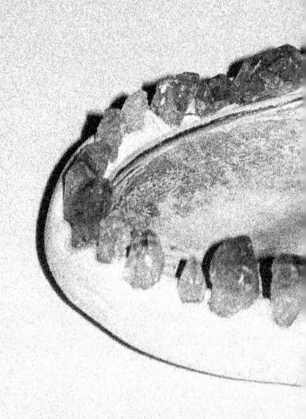

CAROL SHELTON WINES 'WILD THING' OLD VINE ZINFANDEL

Mendocino County, USA

WINE AROMA WHEEL

'If people say they can't smell, they don't have the words.' Ann Noble, professor at the University of California at Davis, was sick and tired of wine drinkers not knowing how to describe the taste of what they were drinking. That's why she invented the Aroma Wheel: an easy tool to describe a wine that moved from general terms (fruity) to smaller categories (berry fruit, tropical fruit, citrus fruit) and finally to more specific flavours (blackberry, pineapple, lemon).

Carol Shelton knew from an early age that she wanted to become a winemaker. During her oenology studies at UC Davis, she majored in Fermentation Science under the tutelage of Ann Noble. Carol made her first harvest in 1978, and is now an award-winning, pioneering winemaker who is based in California and specialised in a single grape: zinfandel.

YOU
MAKE
MY HEART
SING

Carol Shelton makes this wine under the
motto: 'you are what you drink'. 'Wild
Thing' gets its name on the one hand from
the wild-looking 60-year-old bush vines,
and on the other hand from the wild yeast
that has been used to make this wine.
Although grapes do have natural yeast on
their skin that can start fermentation, it
is more common to add man-made yeasts when
a wine is made.

So let's come up with a description of
this wine based on Ann Noble's Aroma
Wheel, since that knowledge is part of its
oenological heritage. The 'Wild Thing'
Old Vine Zinfandel is *fruity*, leaning
towards *tree fruit* such as *cherry*, but
also containing flavours of *berry* ¬- more
specifically *raspberry*, as well as some
dried or cooked fruit, like *strawberry
jam*. It is *woody* in a *resinous* way with
notes of *tobacco*, *cedar* and *vanilla*. In
terms of texture and body, the wine is
smooth and round with a long finish.

DOOVY

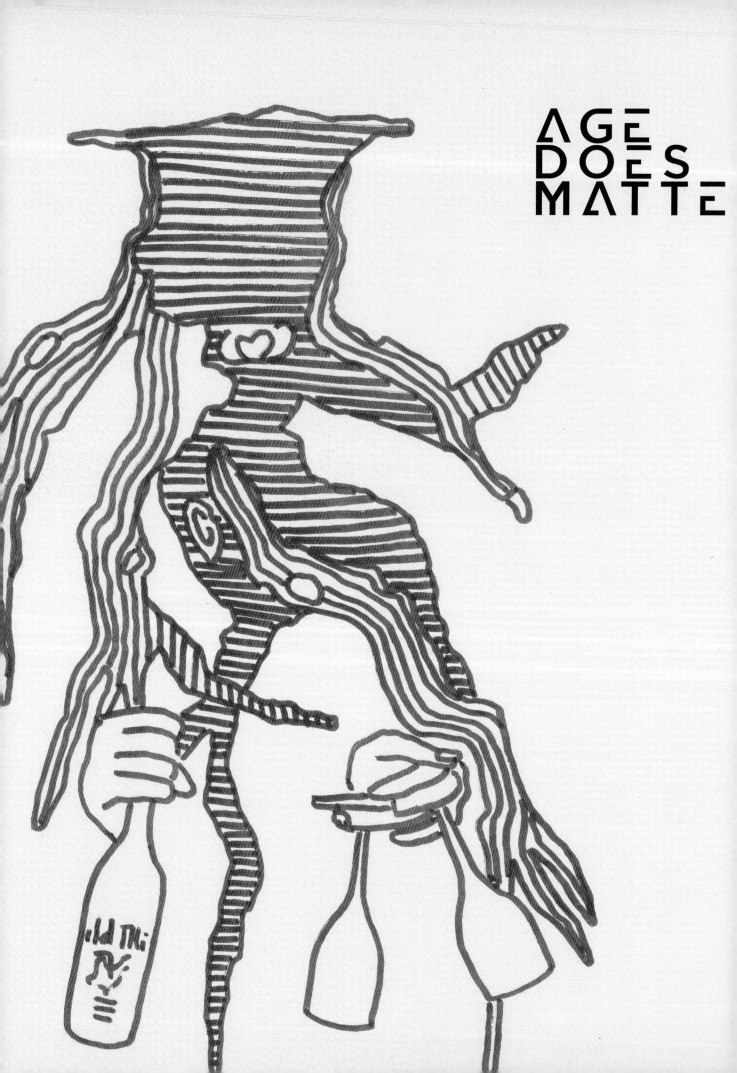

AGE
DOES
MATTE

The label of this wine shows an old vine. Grapevines have a lifespan nearly as long as that of human beings, and their phases of development also show some similarities. In their early years, they don't produce any fruit yet. Once they move past a certain point, the older they get, the less productive they become. Still, it must be said that listening to the stories told by an elderly grandparent or tasting a wine made from older vines is often more meaningful. The conversations may be less loud, but have more depth.

Known as 'old vines' in California, they are called '*vieilles vignes*' in France. These types of vines give low yields, but produce wines that are very interesting in terms of quality. The only question is, when can you start calling your vines old? There is no legislation on this anywhere in the world. In the case of the Old Vines Zinfandel, the grapes come from vines that are sixty years old.

REAL AMERICAN HERO

For years, it was believed that zinfandel was an indigenous grape, America's national pride. However, it was discovered in the 1990s with the help of DNA research that this grape did not in fact originate in the United States. What the Americans know as zinfandel initially came from Croatia, where the grape is referred to as *tribidrag* – but it is also found throughout Puglia, and is better known under its Italian name: primitivo.

Zinfandel, tribidrag and primitivo: all one and the same grape. When they heard in Puglia that their primitivo was the same grape, they decided to label their wines intended for export to America under the name zinfandel. The relabelling was initially banned by the US Bureau of Alcohol, Tobacco and Firearms due to insufficient evidence. In the end, research confirmed the resemblance. And the university where they came to this conclusion? UC Davis!

ANNE &
JEAN-FRANCOIS
GANEVAT
LE JAJA DU BEN

Jura, France

L'ENFANT TERRIBLE DU JURA

Jean-François Ganevat is considered the Jura superstar — the kind of wine producer who pretty much single-handedly put the region on the map. As a young winemaker, he worked for nine years as cellar master at Jean-Marc Morey in Chassagne-Montrachet (Burgundy). Having learned all the tricks from the old maestro, Albert Morey, he decided to return home in 1998 and take over the helm of the family business, a tradition dating back to 1650. After all, Jean-François Ganevat is the fourteenth generation in a family of winemakers.

Jean-François Ganevat's style is uncompromising; doubt does not exist in his mindset. He always works biodynamically and in the most natural way possible, and the results are impressive. His many different wines (including his Cuvée de l'Enfant Terrible) are sought after all over the world, often sold out even before they are bottled. In all the wines made by Jean-François Ganevat, you can taste the link to Burgundy. He makes nearly 100 different crus — per year, that is! Produced from only 13 hectares of vineyard, the demand for Jean-François Ganevat's wines is greater than the supply. How do you solve that?

BROTHER AND SISTER

After all these years in Burgundy, Jean-François Ganevat had long since learned how to make more wine without being limited by the size of his domain. And so, in 2014, he founded a trading company (*société de négoce*) with his sister Anne. In the meantime, he had already found a group of ten grape farmers who work according to the same strict requirements as he does.

One of the grape farmers is called Benoit, and 'Le Jaja du Ben' (short for Benoit) is made from his grapes. The label was designed by Anne Ganevat and shows a man drinking a glass of red wine. Is it Benoit? Is it Jean-François? No, it is just a figure drawn from her imagination.

JURASSIC GLOU GLOU

Because his family business has such a long, rich history, Jean-François Ganevat not only has vineyards with old vines, but also a number of vineyards planted with grape varieties that have long been banned under the appellation of the Jura. This includes petit béclan, gros béclan, gueuche (both blanc and noir), seyve-villard, corbeau, portugais bleu, enfariné, argant and poulsard blanc. Ancient grapes well known for their elegance, light tannins (in the black grapes) and extreme drinkability, locally referred to as *'vins de glou-glou'*. Due to the restrictions of the appellation, they come to market declassified simply as Vin de France.

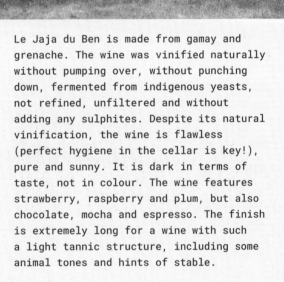

Le Jaja du Ben is made from gamay and grenache. The wine was vinified naturally without pumping over, without punching down, fermented from indigenous yeasts, not refined, unfiltered and without adding any sulphites. Despite its natural vinification, the wine is flawless (perfect hygiene in the cellar is key!), pure and sunny. It is dark in terms of taste, not in colour. The wine features strawberry, raspberry and plum, but also chocolate, mocha and espresso. The finish is extremely long for a wine with such a light tannic structure, including some animal tones and hints of stable.

SEX SELLS

As is the case with all enfants terribles, Jean-François Ganevat is not impeccable. His wines J'en Veux!!! ('I want some'), J'en Veux Encore!!! ('I want some more') and De Toute Beauté Nature ('all of nature's beauty') came to market with labels that have been described as sexist. Their labels feature drawings of nude or semi-nude female figures, including one woman with her hand in her pants.

Sex sells. That's a fact, even now. All the wines of Jean-François Ganevat sell out every year – including the ones with labels that are seen as shocking. Ultimately, it is the quality of the wine in the bottle that determines how great the demand for this product is.

Le Jaja du Ben

ET
BIM!
ROUGE

Côtes de Gascogne France

AND
BOOM!

Not only the name Et Bim!, but also
the style of the label is reminiscent
in every respect of the pop art made
famous by Roy Lichtenstein. This includes
the comic strip style with classic Ben
Day dots and the use of bright, mostly
primary colours, outlined in bold black.
The only thing that's missing on this
label is a speech balloon. Even the name
Et Bim! translates as 'And Boom!'

Roy Lichtenstein (1923-1997) was a New
York-based pop artist from an affluent
Jewish family. He served in the US army
from 1943 until 1946 before completing
his Master of Fine Arts degree in
1949. Advertisements and cartoons
often inspired his work. Lichtenstein
replaced the mechanical reproduction of
the cartoon with the painter's manual
work. The subjects of his art are mainly
emotionally powerful themes, such as war
and love.

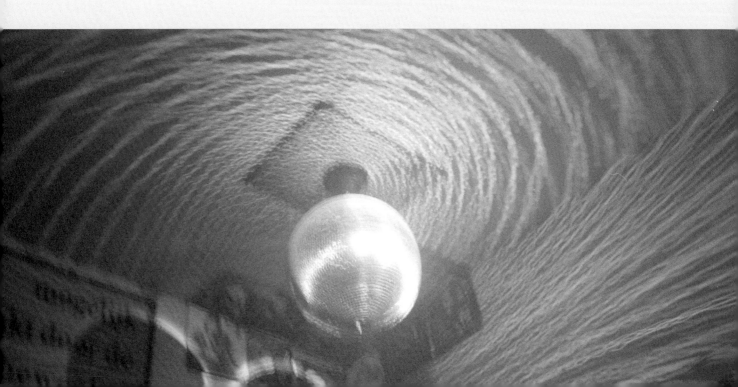

EVERY DAY DRINKING WINE

Et Bim! comes from the Côtes de Gascogne in the south-western part of France, the region between Bordeaux, Toulouse and the Pyrenees. This red wine is made from the grapes merlot, cabernet and tannat. The merlot and cabernet are both from Bordeaux, while tannat is widely planted in the nearby appellations of Madiran and Béarn. The tannic wines of this grape — the name tannat derives from tannins — do indeed go perfectly with a grilled steak served with Béarnaise sauce.

The wine itself is not as exciting as the label suggests. See it as your everyday drinking wine that is decent, affordable and drinkable, with cassis, blackberries, liquorice and bay leaf. Feel free to compare Et Bim! with an entry-level Bordeaux, but with a slightly thicker tannin structure due to the addition of the tannat. According to the label on the back, it is your perfect companion to tapas, grilled red meats or poultry.

The producer of the Et Bim! wines is Diou Biban (DBB) Club, a company specialising in making wine from grapes that come not only from the south-west of France, but also from Spain and Portugal. DBB Club has wines from Toro and Castilla y Léon in its portfolio, as well as Portuguese table wines, port and even gin.

In addition to the south-west French Et Bim! wines, the company also makes local wines that are marketed more traditionally. They also come from the Côtes de Gascogne or the nearby appellations of Madiran (red only) and Pacherenc du Vic-Bilh for white. The Et Bim! wines are also available in rosé, dry white or semi-sweet 'moelleux'.

HOLD OR DRINK?

The label of the Et Bim! wines specifies a three-year drinking window. But how long can you actually keep a wine? The answer to this question differs per wine and depends on four factors: tannins, alcohol, sugars and acidity.

Let's check it out. The wines that you can hold in storage for extended periods are, for example, strongly tannic wines such as Bordeaux, Barolo and Rioja. Wines that have a long life due to their high alcohol content are Amarone della Valpolicella, port and sherry. Examples of noble sweet wines with a large amount of residual sugars are Sauternes, Tokaji and Trockenbeerenauslese (as well as Beerenauslese, Eiswein and Auslese). The wines that can be stored for longer due to their acidity are often made from the grapes riesling, grüner veltliner or chenin blanc. If you don't know whether you can hold a wine or should drink it as young as possible, look at the colour of the bottle glass. In general, the darker the glass, the longer you can store the wine away. Wines don't like sunlight, unless they are already poured into your glass.

170 / 171

SERRAGGHIA
FANINO
CALABRATTO
E PHANTELLO

Pantelleria, Italy

"Holy shit, what the fuck is this?" A shocked exclamation like that could well be your first reaction when you pour a glass of Serragghia 'Fanino' Catarratto e Pignatello. The wine looks nothing like what you are used to seeing: it is cloudy and orange-brown. And that's only logical sense when you consider that it is made in a natural way from an equal mix of white and black grapes: catarratto and pignatello (a.k.a. perricone).

Fanino is a nature wine, although winemaker Gabrio Bini prefers to call it 'natural'. Could this be an orange wine? It looks like it, it tastes like it, but in the purest sense it's not, simply due to the fact that it is not made exclusively from white grapes. The wine ferments long and slowly and ripens in terracotta amphorae. It is surprising, vivid and one of a kind, featuring the taste of blood orange, lychee and wild herbs, including a high acidity and pleasant tension.

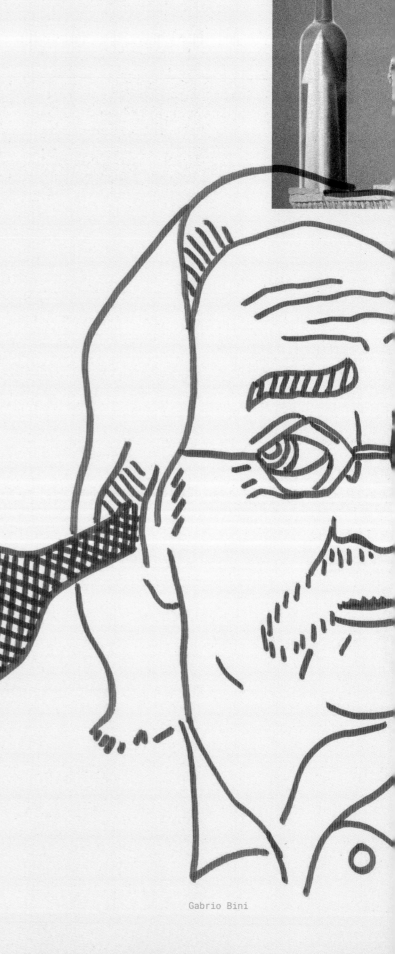

Gabrio Bini

BACK TO THE FUTURE

Owner and winemaker Gabrio Bini is a living legend. With his long grey hair, Gabrio looks a bit like Emmett 'Doc' Brown from the Back to the Future trilogy. He bought Azienda Agricola Serragghia in 1995, but only started selling his wines in 2005. It took him ten years to understand the process of making wines the way he wanted to. In the meantime, he bought more land and expanded his domain from one hectare to its current eight hectares.

Gabrio Bini has an infinite energy and enthusiasm. His winemaking method reinforces the similarities to 'Doc' from Back to the Future, and that includes the choices he makes. Bini was strongly influenced by the way wine was made in Georgia 8,000 years ago. It could be said that his story is an updated edition of Back to the Future, with wine in the starring role.

SECOND CAREER

Originally an architect from Milan, Gabrio Bini now lives in and travels between Pantelleria, Milan and Paris. He runs the family estate together with his wife Geneviève, who is an art director, and their son Giotto. The label of all the Serragghia wines features the upright arrow, a creation by Gabrio Bini himself, of course. In reality, the arrow is a man-sized lamp with a neon light behind it. In the label, the light is used to write the name of the wine.

Gabrio Bini is known for holding his bottle to his ear in photographs, which, thanks to the arrow, creates a strange image. Fans all over the world have been imitating his famous pose on social media. Clearly, the design of the Serragghia wine labels is very photogenic and extremely instagrammable.

'Fanino' Catarratto e Pignatello

BLACK PEARL OF THE MEDITERRANEAN

The wine's official designation of origin is Terre Siciliane IGP. Serragghia is located on the island of Pantelleria, also known as the Black Pearl of the Mediterranean. Officially part of the Sicilian province of Trapani, geographically Pantelleria is closer to Tunisia than Sicily. The island is famous for its capers, its volcanic soil, and its role as a quiet and peaceful holiday destination that is popular with the jet set.

On the other hand, Pantelleria is an island where refugees frequently arrive by boat from Africa. Not in such large numbers as Lampedusa nearby, but still. For example, on New Year's Day 2020, a 20-year-old Tunisian made the 70-kilometre crossing to Pantelleria on the open sea. Pretty dangerous, especially when you consider that thousands of refugees have died in recent years on the boat trip from northern Africa to various Greek and Italian islands.

PARTIDA CREUS XL

Catalunya, Spain

THE
BRA
CLUB

Located in the northern Italian region
of Piemonte — right in between Turin
and Barolo — you will find the city of
Bra: the epicentre of the slow food
movement. This movement is a natural
response to the role that fast food
plays in our society. Slow food is all
about preserving the local culture and
cuisine by using regional products.
That includes farming practices and
livestock, but also seeds and crops.
The international symbol of slow food
is the snail.

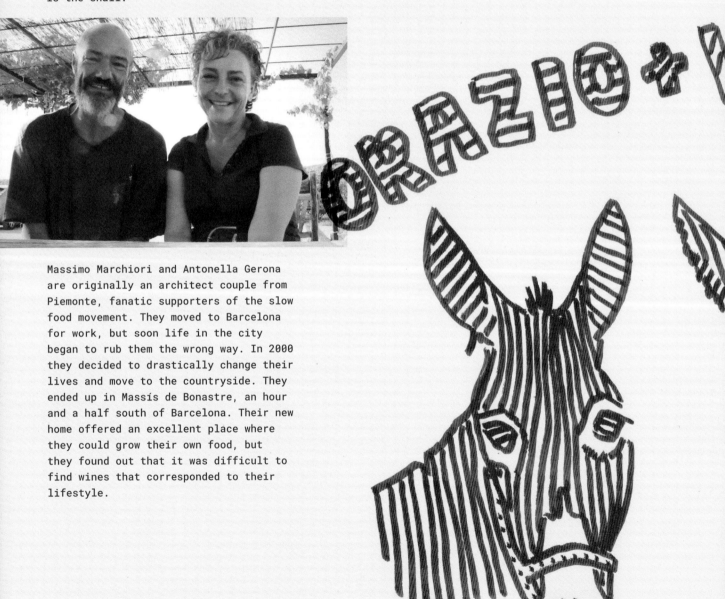

Massimo Marchiori and Antonella Gerona
are originally an architect couple from
Piemonte, fanatic supporters of the slow
food movement. They moved to Barcelona
for work, but soon life in the city
began to rub them the wrong way. In 2000
they decided to drastically change their
lives and move to the countryside. They
ended up in Massís de Bonastre, an hour
and a half south of Barcelona. Their new
home offered an excellent place where
they could grow their own food, but
they found out that it was difficult to
find wines that corresponded to their
lifestyle.

INEYARD
UNTERS

Entirely in alignment with the
principles of the slow food movement,
Massimo and Antonella decided to make
their own wines. As soon as they got the
chance, they bought up nearby vineyards,
but they also looked for deserted
vineyards in the area that they could
lease. They regularly drove up and down
to Barcelona to spot old and neglected
vineyards along the way.

An additional advantage of these plots
is that they are often planted with
very old vines. These give low yields,
but extremely high quality. Moreover,
the vineyards are often planted with
grape varieties from the distant past,
like garrut, vinyater, samso and
queixal de llop. In some cases, local
legislation no longer permits their
use in officially recognised wines.
As a result, they regularly have to
declassify their wines to the lowest
level of table wine.

All this resulted in a wine company that goes by the name Partida Creus, referring to the crosses used in the past to separate companies. In the vineyard, they work without machines. The only help they have is from Orazio and Vincenza, a donkey and a mule. The wines are made in a way that they would be proud of in Bra: the fermentation takes place with the grapes' own yeasts and the wines are bottled in an unfiltered state, without added sulphites.

That makes XL a natural wine with a cloudy look. You immediately discover an apple cider association in the nose: fresh apples with a yeasty aroma. This wine is characterised by a strong acidity. It has a bite, but is funky at the same time. Modern and very popular among millennials – not least due to its culinary versatility in combination with dishes from Ottolenghi's cuisine, such as his roasted cauliflower salad with a dressing based on capers, dill and garlic.

GOT TO BE TRUE TO MYSELF

The label of the wine consists of a single piece. In particular, the front of the label is minimalistic and at the same time striking. All wines from Partida Creus are named using two letters that refer to the grape variety, such as VN (vinel-lo), SM (sumoll), GT (garrut) and this XL: xarel-lo.

Xarel-lo is a grape that is often blended with parellada and macabeo to make cava. Instead, Massimo and Antonella want to focus on the grape on its own. After all, they want to be true to themselves by making natural products that are as pure as they are.

THERE WILL BE NO WORKING DURING DRINKING HOURS

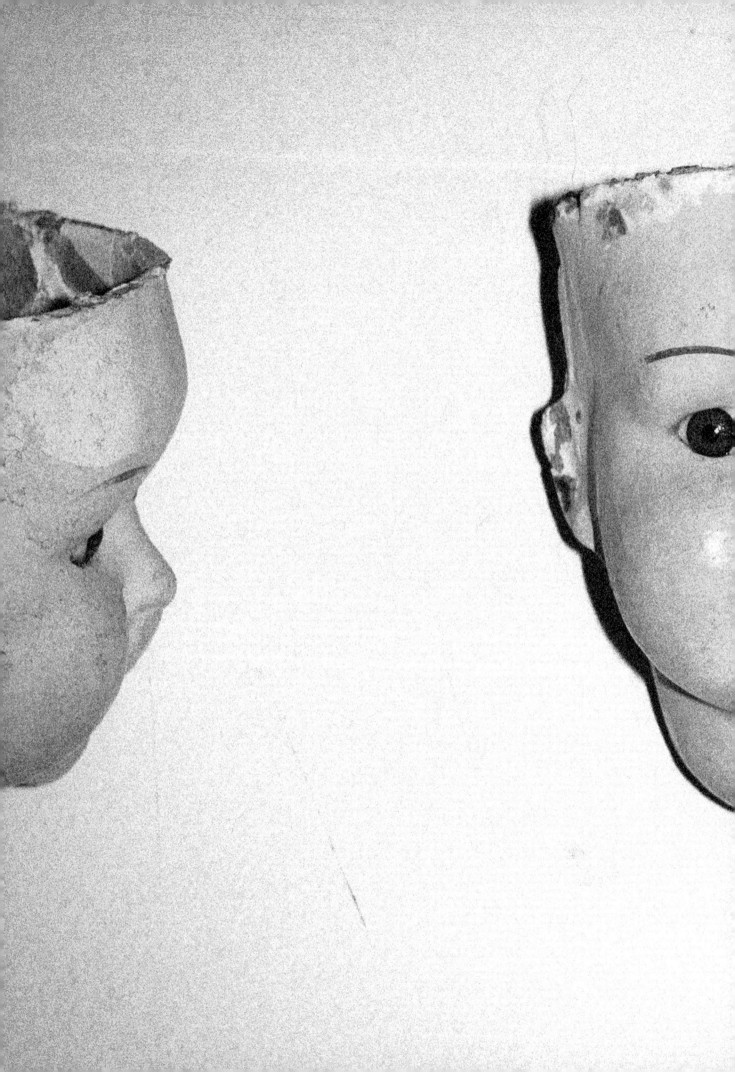

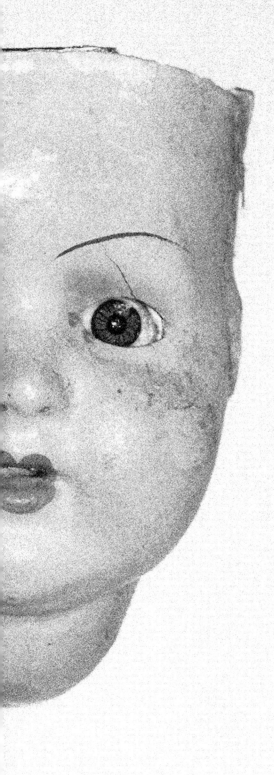

CONCEITO BASTARDO

DOC Douro, Portugal

TROUSSEAU OR BASTARDO?

Bastardo. Interesting name for a wine, isn't it? In this case, it's simply the name of the grape. It originates from the French Jura region, close to the Alps, and is also known under its ampelographic name: trousseau. DNA analyses have proved that they are in fact the same grape. Bastardo is the Portuguese name for this grape, which is also allowed in a traditional port blend. Once the most widely planted grape in the Douro, it has now become a rarity.

The label of this Bastardo was created by Portuguese artist João Noutel, who also works for Niepoort. The label does not give much information about the wine or the winery. In fact, the only word on the front label is Bastardo. The image on the label is disconcerting, alienating. Who should this be? What is it supposed to inspire in us? And why does this person have no real face and two big round holes for eyes? Is this the fate of the bastard? Questions, so many questions...

STOMPED BY FEET

Bastardo is related to the pinot noir, which explains its light colour and gentle tannins. Often bastardo is found in a field blend, but in this case the grapes come from a plot that is 100% bastardo, planted on slate soils. The name of the vineyard is Quinta da Veiga, and the grapevines are thirty years old.

In the production of this wine, the grapes are still traditionally trodden by foot, as is still common at a number of large and famous port houses. Grape-treading is considered better than machines, since feet are softer. The result is sunny, fruity and somewhat elegant with red cherry, raspberry, cranberry, spices, black pepper, liquorice and bay leaves. Soft, round and smooth. And particularly low in alcohol for a Douro table wine: only 12%!

Bastardo Vinho Tinto

CARLA & RITA

WITH LOVE

Bastardo is made by Conceito Wines, a family business run by young winemaker Rita Ferreira Marqués and her mother Carla Costa Ferreira. Their winery is situated in Vila Nova de Foz Côa, located far upstream in the Douro Valley. Conceito has over 80 hectares of vineyard and produces a wide range of different wines, varying from sparkling wines to red and white table wines and port wines.

The name Conceito literally means 'concept'. All the labels of the Conceito wines are conceptually strong and always show at least one circle in the label. In addition to wines from Portugal, Conceito also makes wines in New Zealand and South Africa.

THE MOST FAMOUS BASTARD

Bastardo has a rich history as a Portuguese grape variety, but the most famous wine named after a bastard is from the heart of Burgundy: Bâtard-Montrachet. Le Montrachet is one of the most sought-after Grands Crus in the Côte de Beaune. Its fame has been used to spice up the names of the two villages where Le Montrachet is situated: Chassagne-Montrachet and Puligny-Montrachet.

It was the Lord of Puligny who was responsible for the name of this wine. He divided his land between his eldest son, who was a knight: Le Chevalier. Another part of his land was given to his maiden daughters: Les Pucelles. Finally, there was a piece of land left for his illegitimate son: Le Bâtard. To this very day, we still distinguish the plots of Chevalier Montrachet, Les Pucelles and Bâtard Montrachet, considered to be the world's best and most complex examples of chardonnay. Les Pucelles is classified as Premier Cru and Chevalier Montrachet and Bâtard Montrachet are both classified as Grand Cru.

Viticulturist Nuno Fernandes, chief winemaker Rita Marques and winemaker Manuel Sapage

WEINGUT ESTERHAZY TROCKENBEEREN- AUSLESE

Neusiedlersee, Austria

NOBLE ROT

Trockenbeerenauslese (TBA): the German word literally translates as 'dry-berry select harvest'. It is the king of sweet wines. TBA can be put on par with Sauternes and the best Tokaji. It is even nobler than Eiswein and sweeter than Beerenauslese, Auslese or Spätlese (late harvest). Trockenbeerenauslese is a wine made from raisins that have undergone the process of pourriture noble, edelfäule, muffa nobile or – as they would say in English – noble rot. The official name for this phenomenon is *botrytis cinerea*.

Once the botrytis fungus affects the fruit, the water content in the grape decreases. This increases the sugar content in the grape. In addition, botrytis gives the eventual wine an extra flavour dimension, often recognisable in the form of orange marmalade, pure nectar and raisins.

LIQUID GOLD

This sweet wine is amber-coloured, orangey-brown. It is extremely viscous in texture and offers a wide range of flavours. The characteristic botrytis touch can be tasted as honey and dried apricots. In addition, you can use the full recipe for an apple pie as a tasting note: caramelised apples, raisins, dough, cinnamon, vanilla and a hint of lemon juice. Thanks to its high acidity and sugar content, this wine has an infinite life.

The Esterházy Trockenbeerenauslese Welschriesling 2015 contains 216 grams of residual sugar per litre. In comparison: that is more than twice as much as Coca-Cola, which contains 'only' 106 grams of residual sugar per litre. Because of its sweetness, TBA is often seen as a dessert wine. Of course you can serve it with a tarte-tatin or other pastry with fruit, but the combination with the ever-controversial foie gras or pungent blue cheeses is more exciting. In actual fact, however, there is no perfect wine and food pairing predestined for TBA. Instead, it is best served as an alternative to dessert.

A WELCOME GUEST

On the label you will find an image of Maria Theresa of Austria (1717-1780). She was reigning Archduchess of Austria and Queen of Hungary and Bohemia. In the 650-year-long Habsburg dynasty, she was the only woman to take the throne. She was also the mother of sixteen children, including Marie-Antoinette ('Let them eat cake'), for whom she diligently arranged a marriage to the future king of France: Louis XVI. Little did she know that Marie-Antoinette would be beheaded at the Place de la Concorde in Paris in 1793 at the age of 37.

Maria Theresa was a welcome guest at Schloss Esterházy in Eisenstadt, the provincial capital of Burgenland. She was on excellent terms with Nikolaus I, Prince Esterházy. He was a military officer in Austrian service and also the employer of one of the most famous and influential composers of classical music: Joseph Haydn.

Joseph Haydn

SO LONG FAREWELL AUF WIEDERSEHEN

The history of the noble Hungarian family of Esterházy dates back to the 13th century. The family was known for its exorbitant lifestyle and great interest in art, science, architecture, music and wine. With more than 250 years of history as a wine producer and 90 hectares of vineyard, Weingut Esterházy today calls itself the most modern wine estate in Austria.

The ties between Prince Nikolaus and Joseph Haydn seem to have been excellent. Haydn, for example, regularly received gold ducats for his compositions. Moreover, he was paid part of his wages in wine, and his mistress and his younger brother, a mediocre vocalist, were also on Esterházy's payroll. Yet there was occasionally friction, as can be seen from Symphony no. 45. When this 'Farewell' symphony was first performed in Eszterháza, the Hungarian summer palace, the musicians stopped one by one during the last adagio, blew out their candles and left the stage. It was a protest to show that the musicians did not want to be away from home that long in the summer, but would have much preferred to stay with their families in Eisenstadt.

Trockenbeerenauslese

DOC Douro, Portugal

TABLE WINE FROM THE DOURO

The story of Niepoort started in 1842 when Franciscus Marius van der Niepoort (born in the Dutch city of Hilversum) came to Porto, where he launched a business as a port trader. When he died in 1887, the company still has no land or vineyards. Still family-owned today, the company is in the hands of Dirk van der Niepoort, fifth-generation winemaker.

When Dirk joined his father Rolf in the family business in 1987, it was finally time for the company to buy its own vineyards: Quinta de Nápoles and Quinta do Carril. Now that Niepoort owned its own vineyards, their business also expanded from port to table wine. These wines were still from the Douro and still made from port grapes bearing such local names as touriga franca, tinta roriz, tinta amarela, touriga nacional and tinto cão.

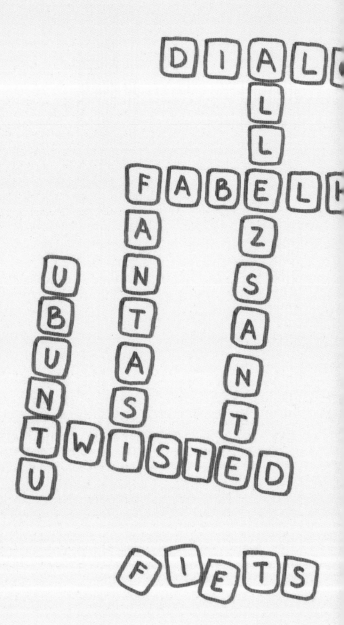

ABSOLUTELY FABULOUS

Although Dirk van der Niepoort dreamt of making an elegant table wine from his Douro grapes, Robustus 1990, his first wine, was a monster. His father Rolf was his biggest critic and didn't like the wine at all. When Dirk went on a trip to Australia in 1991, his father decided to sell 80% of the wine. On his return, Dirk found out that he had only 720 bottles left of his first vintage. When he served the wine to Michael Broadbent, the most influential wine critic at that time, Broadbent gave it the best possible compliment and described it as 'the Latour of Portugal'. But Dirk's father's opinion never changed; Rolf always complained: "It smells of shit".

In 2004 Niepoort launched a project for the German market to introduce German wine consumers to Douro table wine. The project and the name of the wine were called Fabelhaft ('fabulous'). An entry-level red table wine made of Douro grapes decorated with a label inspired by German cartoonist avant la lettre Wilhelm Busch. The project was a success, inspiring Niepoort to expand to other markets with their own names and matching labels. Fabelaktig (Norway), Fantasi (Denmark), Allez Santé (Belgium), Diálogo (Portugal), Drink Me (UK), Twisted (USA), Ubuntu (South Africa) and Gestolen Fiets (Netherlands).

Gestolen Fiets

A LOGISTICAL NIGHTMARE

Like all the original Fabelhaft wines, the Dutch edition had its own label. The first version for the Gestolen Fiets (which translates as 'stolen bicycle') included artwork by Dutch cartoonist Willem Holtrop. The current cartoon on the label is the work of Peter van Straaten (1935-2016), an artist known for sketches showing people in awkward situations. The caption of the cartoon translates as "we should do this more often" and can be explained in several ways. Does it have anything to do with the bike ride? Is it about the act of drinking a glass of wine? Or does it hint at sexual innuendo, suggesting something that has happened or is about to happen? There is plenty of room for interpretation.

The Fabelhaft project with all its different artists, labels and language-related sales markets was a worldwide success. Or, as Niepoort himself says: a rewarding project, but a logistical nightmare: one wine, fifteen different appearances. To make the story even more challenging logistically, there is also a white version of this wine that is sold in various countries.

JE SUIS NIEPOORT

Gestolen Fiets is inviting, charming, vivid and straightforward with jammy black forest fruit, blackberry and liquorice tones. Sunny, juicy and persistent. The wine has an extremely high drinkability.

Peter van Straaten died in 2016. His predecessor on the label, Willem Holtrop, narrowly escaped death just one year earlier. He was travelling to Paris for a meeting with the editors of one of his clients. His client was Charlie Hebdo, and Willem Holtrop was on his way to that office on the day of the terrorist attack.

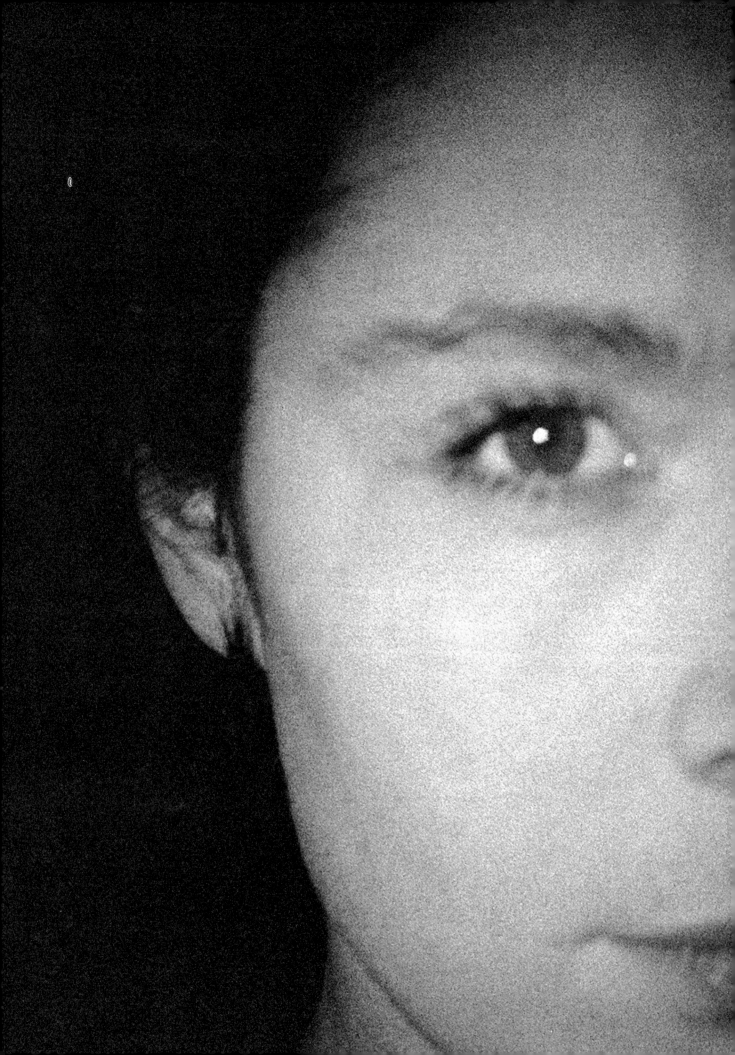

TESTALONGA
BABY BANDITO
KEEP ON PUNCHING

Swartland, South Africa

IL BANDITO TESTALONGA

Testalonga. Doesn't sound very South African, does it? The name originates from Antonino Di Blasi (1728-1767), a.k.a. Il Bandito Testalonga, a legendary bandit of the 18th century. The Robin Hood of Sicily who stole from the rich to feed the poor, he was said to be a gentleman rover with a noble soul. Il Bandito Testalonga was notorious and relentless. He used to sign his kidnappings with cuts on the ears and on the tip of the nose, depending on the intensity of the extortion requests. Although his actions were quite controversial, he is still considered a hero in Sicily.

Testalonga is also the nickname of Antonio Perrino, the winemaker of the first skin-fermented white wine that Craig Hawkins ever tasted in his life. Hawkins was impressed and asked Perrino if he could use his alias for the name of his wine farm.

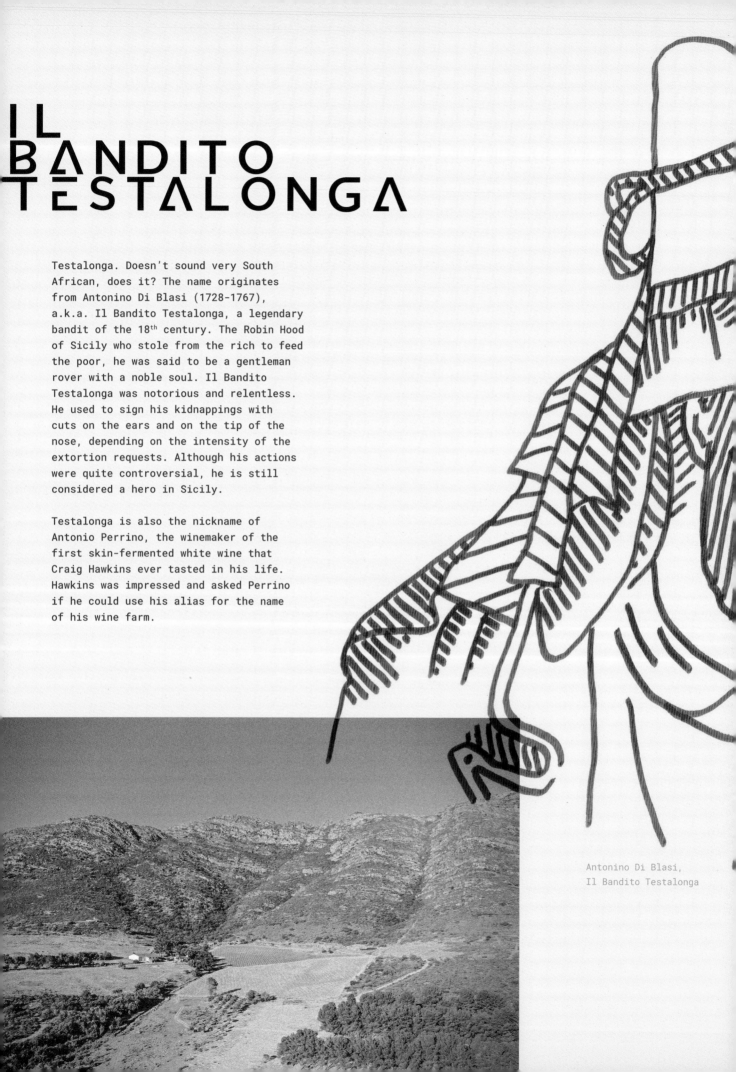

Antonino Di Blasi,
Il Bandito Testalonga

LOCAL HERO

Craig Hawkins is a South African winemaker. As an enfant terrible and pioneer, he is often misunderstood by the international press – perhaps simply because his wines cannot be categorised. Hawkins works organically, using almost biodynamic principles, and makes his wines as natural as possible. It could almost be considered a no-intervention approach. The result is a totally new concept for South African wines. Add the name Testalonga to that, and you'll understand who we are dealing with here: a local hero from Swartland.

As a child, Craig used to work in the cellar of his brother Neil Hawkins, who is now a winemaker in Gippsland, Australia. After university Craig worked as a cellar hand for former surfer and Swartland celebrity winemaker Eben Sadie. In the meantime, he went to Europe for several work internships, including one at Dirk Niepoort (Douro, Portugal) and one at Tom Lubbe. A New Zealander who grew up in South Africa, Lubbe currently runs Domaine Matassa in the French Roussillon, a wine estate which is well known for its *vin nature*.

SUPER
SIZE
ME

All his traveling, learning from
and meeting up with other winemakers
influenced Craig Hawkins and the way he
viewed wines. He soon knew he wanted to
make natural wines. Over-manipulated wines
make Hawkins unhappy: "It's like eating
McDonald's food."

The Baby Bandito Keep On Punching is an
unoaked single vineyard Swartland chenin
blanc. Wild-fermented, unfiltered and with
minimal sulphites, the wine is funky,
obscure and quaint. Floral and slightly
yeasty with yellow apple, dried hay, straw
and honey, it offers excellent acidity,
crisp, chill and succulent. Think of it as
a mixture between Craig Hawkins' favourite
musicians: Bob Marley, Eminem and Mozart.

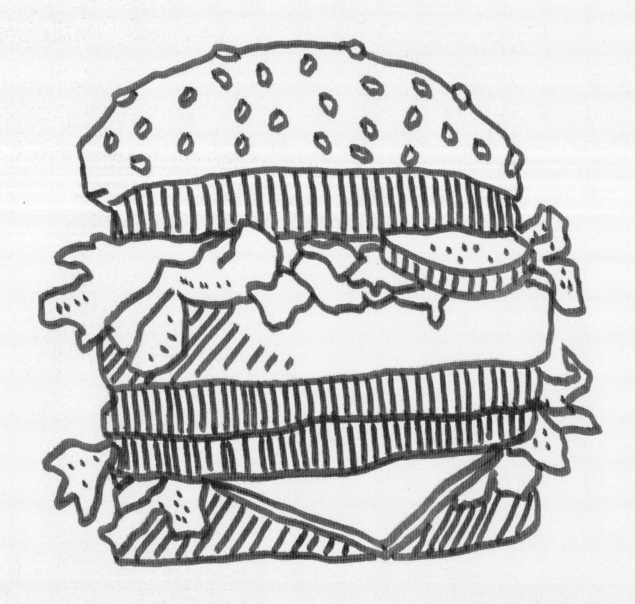

KEEP ON PUNCHING

Craig and his wife Carla now live in Bandits Kloof in Swartland. Their wines are brought to market in two ranges: El Bandito and Baby Bandito. The Baby Bandito wines are all named after an encouragement that you would give to a child: Follow Your Dreams (carignan), Stay Brave (chenin blanc, orange wine) and Keep On Punching.

The name Keep On Punching originates from "Keep on punching, the head will fall", an expression used by Professor Lyal White, a former hockey mate of Craig Hawkins. White used to say this at half-time during their hockey matches. Lyal White, founding senior director of the Johannesburg Business School, is also the photographer of the label for El Bandito King of Grapes. The photo on the label of the Baby Bandito range, however, is an image of a street child in Vietnam taken from a snapshot by Craig Hawkins' brother, Mark.

CATENA ZAPATA
MALBEC
ARGENTINO

Mendoza, Argentina

THE STORY OF MALBEC

The label tells the history of malbec, which also became the poster for a play written by a Catena family member. It is an authentic theatrical production that has been performed in theatres in London, Amsterdam and other major European cities where Catena sells a fair share of their wines, as well as Latin America and the United States. The plot is about four women who together tell the story of malbec: Eleanor of Aquitaine, the immigrant, phylloxera and Adrianna Catena.

The story goes a little something like this. Duchess *Eleanor of Aquitaine* loved her malbec grape so much that she obliged all vintners to grow malbec in Bordeaux and Cahors. *The immigrant* is Ana Mosceta, wife of Nicola Catena. Ana came to Argentina from the poor Le Marche region in Italy. Other immigrants brought the malbec grape to her new land. In the meantime, the devastating grape louse *phylloxera* had destroyed most of Europe's precious vineyards. *Adrianna Catena* represents the opportunities of the New World that made malbec a success in Argentina.

ELEANOR OF AQUITAINE

Eleanor of Aquitaine was the only person who ever lived who became Queen of both France and England. At the age of fifteen, she became the Duchess of Aquitaine, a country one-third the size of current France. She married Louis, the King of France's son, whose father died a year later — making him king and her queen of France. In the meantime, Eleanor had grown to love her black wine made from malbec, which increased its popularity at the French court over the refined wines from the Loire Valley and Burgundy.

After fifteen years of marriage, she divorced at the age of thirty. Eight weeks later, she remarried to Henry II, Duke of Normandy. Within two years, Henry had become King of England, with Eleanor as his queen. This meant that the highly fashionable wines of the regions Bordeaux (and Cahors) fell under English control. And here we have found the link between England and Bordeaux. To the present day, Bordeaux wines are inseparably connected with England and appreciated by English wine lovers.

Malbec Argentino

PHYLLOXER
PART I

Dr Laura Catena

The grape louse, *phylloxera vastatrix*, came from the United States to Europe in the late 1800s. Grape plants are categorised into different families. The American vines (*vitis labrusca*) have natural defences against the root-eating louse, but the European vines (*vitis vinifera*) never stood a chance. The insects devastated most of the roots of the vines. In France alone, 70% of all vineyards were destroyed.

The problem came from the US, and so did the solution: European grapevines were grafted onto American rootstocks. This method is still used today in almost every vineyard in the world. With the replanting of the vineyards in the beginning of the 20th century, most producers decided to exchange their malbec grapes for the nobler cabernet franc or merlot. Malbec with its rusty tannins and dark colour had given their wines the ability to travel in the past, but this was no longer needed because of the rise of railway transportation and steamboats. Malbec was declining in popularity...

FROM ZERO TO HERO

At the other end of the world, in Argentina, winemakers discovered that malbec made outstanding, bold and fruit-forward wines. The grape seemed to need a dry season, which is the case in Mendoza. The vines here get their water from melting snow from the Andes mountain peaks.

Since 1902, the Catena Zapata winery has been a family business, currently managed by Dr Laura Catena. She is the fourth generation, sister to Adrianna Catena and daughter of the famous Nicolás Catena Zapata. The Malbec Argentino is one of the flagship wines of Catena. Made from old wines from the Angélica vineyard and the Nicasia vineyard, it tells a story of a grape dating back more than eight centuries.

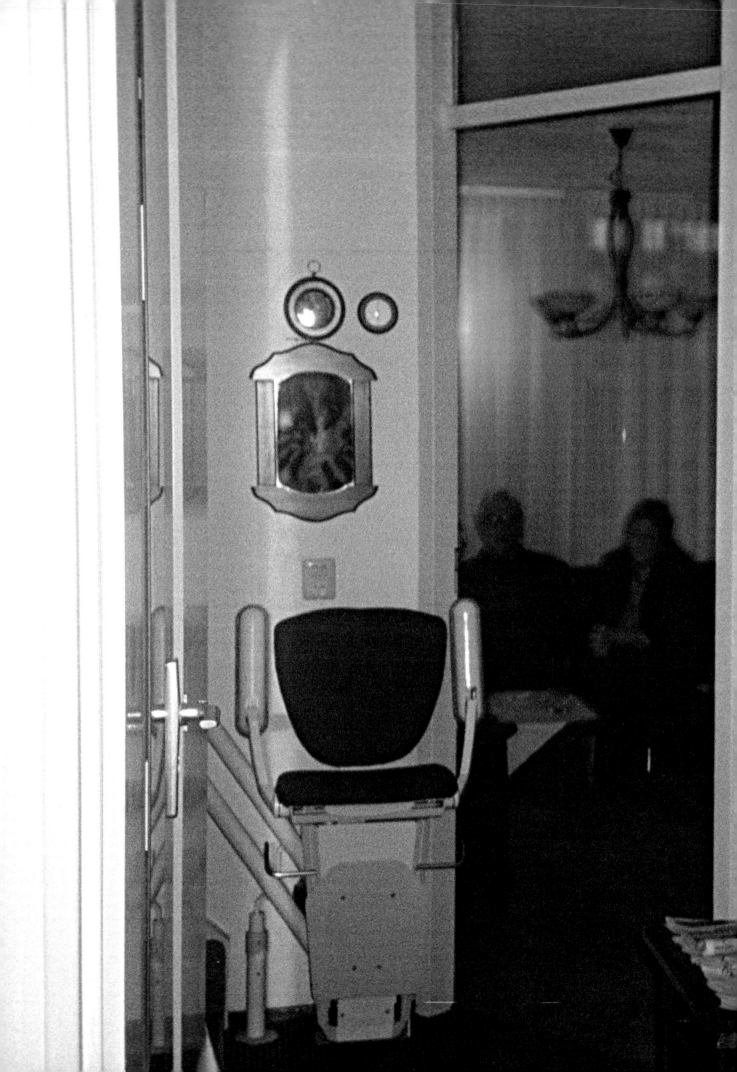

BODEGA
MATSU
EL RECIO

DO Toro, Spain

PHYLLOXERA PART II

After the invention of the steamboat, our world became easier to travel. Since we could, we all did. But like today, intensive travel is not always good for nature. Around 1860, the devastating grape louse *phylloxera vastatrix* entered European vineyards. It is likely that the louse came from America and found its way via London to Bordeaux. In those days, there was a lively connection between the ports of those two cities.

Vintners immediately understood that something was wrong. But just like Covid-19 the infection's spread turned out to be inevitable. "Look what I found on my grape roots!" was the first reaction of a vintner while standing in his neighbouring vineyards. From Bordeaux to other regions in France, and then moving on to Spain, Italy and all other European vineyards, phylloxera devastated a total of 700,000 hectares. To compare: this is almost as much as all the vineyards in France today, or six times the total of all vineyards in South Africa.

DO TORO

After Europe's fate, the rest of the world had been warned. Many regions tightened quarantine rules regarding fruit import. Even today, wine regions with vines that lack American rootstock are at risk of being destroyed by phylloxera. Despite this knowledge, there are some regions that have never been affected by phylloxera. The isolated Canary Islands are a logical exception, but Chile has also escaped infection. Oceans, mountains, deserts and glaciers form the country's natural barriers, making it way too much effort for the grape louse to get there.

The vineyards of the DO Toro are a special case, and have remained intact. This small but ancient Spanish region has been producing wine for more than 2000 years. Situated between Valladolid and Zamora close to the Portuguese border, the Toro vineyards are at a high altitude: 700 meter above sea level, and the soil is rich in sand. The region has a continental climate with Atlantic influences, causing excessive temperatures ranging from -11 in winter to 37 degrees Celsius in summer. No wonder phylloxera kept away from Toro!

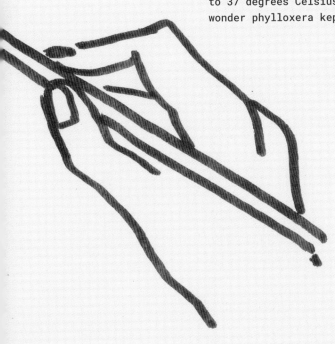

RULES ARE MEANT TO BE BROKEN

As a result, DO Toro has a large number of pre-phylloxera vines — not only older European grapevines, but also, and very exceptionally, European vines growing from European rootstock. Depending on the wine, Bodegas Matsu uses grapevines varying in age from 80 to 110 years old. Wine plants are just like human beings: they can grow old, but they will produce less fruit the older they get. Is that a bad thing? On the contrary! Less fruit means more flavour, more power and more concentrated intensity, ideal for producing top wines. In fact, the wines do not even have to ripen on oak barrels for very long to get their strength and complexity.

Just like in Spain's flagship region of Rioja, the local legislation in Toro dictates the amount of time a wine must age before it is labelled Joven (young wine), Roble (aged between three and six months), Crianza (aged for two years of which at least six months in oak barrels), Reserva (aged for three years of which a minimum of one year in oak barrels) or Gran Reserva (aged for five years of which a minimum of two years in oak barrels). Often the comparison is made with the phases of a person's life. A young wine is a young man and a Grand Reserva is the grandfather of the family.

A FAMILY OF WINES

Bodega Matsu makes all of these wines without actually naming them according to the official rules. Instead they call them El Picaro (the villain), El Recio (the tough guy) and El Viejo (the old man). Their distinctive faces can be seen on the label of each wine.

All wines are made from 100% tinta del toro, the local name for tempranillo. Grapes are grown according to biodynamic principles, but the wines are not officially certified. Why should they? At Matsu, they do not follow the rules. In the meantime, El Recio can easily be compared with a Reserva.

El Recio

Bodega Matsu

COMPAÑIA
DE VINOS
TELMO RODRIGUEZ
GABA DO XIL
BRANCO

DO Valdeorras, Spain

THE
DRIVING
WINEMAKER

For many years, Telmo Rodríguez has been
seen as Spain's rising star. In the
decades since his start, he has become
established as a groundbreaking winemaker
and is considered one of the leaders of
the Spanish quality revolution. Telmo
studied in Bordeaux, learned more in
the Rhône and became a winemaker at
his father's estate in Rioja. But Telmo
wanted to explore more and needed to work
on his own projects.

Nowadays he lives in Madrid, driving out
from there to his company's different
projects. This makes him the Dennis
Bergkamp of the flying winemakers:
the *driving* winemaker. Over the years,
Telmo became involved in more and more
projects, resulting in the ownership of
355 small plots spread all over Spain:
from Rioja, Ribera del Duero, Rueda and
Toro to Valdeorras, Cigales, Cebreros,
Alicante and Malaga. In total Compañía de
Vinos Telmo Rodríguez owns 80 hectares in
Spain, planted with 43 different native
grape varieties.

EVENING OF SIL

Valdeorras is the easternmost region of Galicia, located north of Portugal on the banks of the river Sil (Xil is its ancient name). Valdeorras is the oldest wine region in Galicia and was planted with vines after the ancient Romans finished mining the area for gold; its name literally means Valley of Gold. Telmo Rodríguez was attracted to the valley because of an abandoned vineyard that was thought to be lost after the phylloxera epidemic hit Spain in the nineteenth century. When Telmo first entered the vineyards, it was in the evening. 'Gaba' is the Basque word for evening, hence the name of the wine. Apart from the Branco, there is also a Tinto version of the Gaba do Xil, made from the thick-skinned local grape known as mencía.

Like all the wines of Telmo Rodríguez, Gaba do Xil Branco is organically grown, but not certified. The wine is pure and fruit-driven with yellow apple, pear drops and grapefruit. It is light, juicy and floral with hints of almonds and a slight bitter note. This is your everyday drinking wine that never gets boring, a perfect cool-climate house wine with excellent drinkability.

BUILDING BRIDGES

All packaging for the wines produced
by Compañía de Vinos Telmo Rodríguez
is designed by London-based Fernando
Gutiérrez, who worked for organisations
such as El País, Museo Nacional del
Prado, Benetton, Hermès and Tate Modern.
The story goes that his earlier label
design (with twelve bridges) received
some constructive criticism from one of
the world's best construction engineers,
Mike Schlaich. Fernando Gutiérrez then
redesigned the label — this time with
nine bridges, based on sketches provided
by Mike Schlaich.

The idea behind the bridges on the
label comes from the different plots
where the grapes are grown. The plots
are divided between various places
along the banks of the Río Sil. As a
winemaker, you literally need bridges
to go from one vineyard to another.
More metaphorically, Telmo Rodríguez is
the man who builds bridges between the
modern consumer and his ancient Spanish
grape varieties.

Telmo Rodríguez

FOR THE LOVE OF GODELLO

Telmo Rodríguez works a lot with old vineyards planted with bush vines. These grape plants are not guided along trellises, but grow as an independent bush. They stand further from each other, which comes in handy in Spain, where many of the vineyards have to cope with fierce heat. Grapes hang in de shade of their own leaves, which gives more freshness to the eventual wines. Old vines also have a large root system that allows the plant to reach water. The yields of the old bush vines are low, but quality and complexity of the wines benefit.

Gaba do Xil Branco is made from 100% godello: a high-quality ancient white grape with a history that goes back all the way to the 16th century. In the 1970s, godello was almost extinct, but nowadays its popularity is unstoppable. You'll find the grape in Galicia, especially in Valdeorras, but also in Portugal under the name gouveio. Godello wines are an excellent pairing with asparagus, fresh oysters or sushi.

Gaba do Xil Branco

Old bush vines

AZIENDA
AGRICOLA
FRANK
CORNELISSEN
MAGMA

IGP Terre Siciliane, Italy

NO INTERVENTION PLEASE

'Great people, love Italy': that's what US President Trump said… at least until the G7 summit in May 2017. The location where the event took place is the Sicilian town of Taormina, famous for its ancient Greek amphitheatre and its views over the Mediterranean Sea and Mount Etna. With a history dating back over 2,400 years, the streets tend to be quite narrow, especially for the thirty armoured cars of the US president. He therefore insisted that the narrow roads in the city should be widened. It's like demanding the Eiffel Tower should be removed from Paris...

From Taormina, it is only forty kilometres inland to Azienda Agricola Frank Cornelissen. Doesn't sound very Sicilian, does it? Frank originally came from the Belgian city of Hasselt and has a background in wine trading. Twenty years ago, he decided to leave his motherland and settle in Solicchiata on the northern flank of Mount Etna. His winery extends across 25 hectares planted with vines, other fruit and olive trees. His way of winemaking best describes itself as 'no intervention'. Just like the mayor of Taormina, Frank Cornelissen likes to sit back, relax, live and let live.

Frank Cornelissen

GRAND
VIN
MAGMA

In practice, this means that Frank
Cornelissen does as little as possible.
His work in the vineyard is free of
chemicals and organically certified.
Frank strongly believes in a natural
eco-system without human intervention.
In fact he picks the grapes and lets
them turn into wine with the grape's own
yeasts only. He uses no added sulphite
and he doesn't filter the wine. His
main job is to keep the cellars as clean
as possible. Maybe that is the reason
why visitors with strong perfume or
aftershave are not accepted into the
cellar.

The Grand Vin of the domain is Magma
Rosso: a single vineyard, single grape
variety wine with 15% alcohol. The name
of the vineyard (or 'contrada') is
Barbabecchi, located between 870 and 910
metres above sea level. Nerello mascalese
is the name of the grape and the average
age of the vines is over one hundred
years old. Total production of the Magma
Rosso is 1,500 bottles per year. Its
taste? Rich, elegant and full-bodied with
liquorice and oriental spices. Not your
everyday drinking wine...

Magma

MOUNT ETNA

In terms of label, Frank Cornelissen thinks outside the box. Who needs a label when you can paint five letters on the bottle?
M
A
G
M
A

All the necessary information about the wine is on the back label: alcohol percentage, organic certificate, origin and producer. Since the 2016 vintage, the Magma wines have a Near Field Communication (NFC) chip integrated into the back label. This serves as an authenticity certificate, but is also able to provide consumers with extra information about the wine, such as the bottle date and other information that Frank Cornelissen wants to share with you.

LOCAL HERO

The name of the grape, nerello mascalese, means something like 'the black one from Mascali' – where Mascali is the next town driving twenty kilometres south along the Mediterranean Sea from Taormina. This local hero is known for its late-ripening grapes and light-coloured wines with an elegant tannic structure. Nerello mascalese wines tend to have a high acidity. You can drink them young, but they can age beautifully. Well, where have we heard that before?

Nerello mascalese is the pinot noir or the nebbiolo of Sicily. Now take a look at the two original regions where these grapes come from: Burgundy (Côte de Nuits) and Piedmont (Barolo). What is the similarity between Côte de Nuits, Barolo and the north flanks of Mount Etna? They are all famous for their single vineyard wines or Crus. The contrada Barbabecchi can therefore be seen as the Grand Cru of Sicily.

PALMENTO
COSTANZO
BIANCO DI SEI

DOC Etna Bianco, Italy

LAVA IN YOUR CELLAR

From Azienda Agricola Frank Cornelissen
to Cantine Palmento Costanza is a
4-minute drive. In fact, you could
actually walk from one winemaker to the
other. Both their wineries are on the
northern flank of Mount Etna. The reason
for both of these neighbouring wineries
to be in this book is their unique
label. There must be some special energy
released in your mind that makes you
think differently when you live and work
on a volcano.

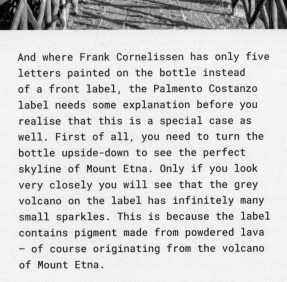

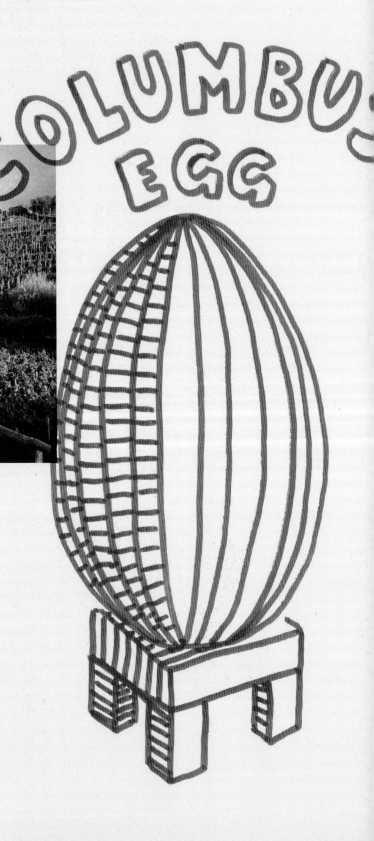

And where Frank Cornelissen has only five
letters painted on the bottle instead
of a front label, the Palmento Costanzo
label needs some explanation before you
realise that this is a special case as
well. First of all, you need to turn the
bottle upside-down to see the perfect
skyline of Mount Etna. Only if you look
very closely you will see that the grey
volcano on the label has infinitely many
small sparkles. This is because the label
contains pigment made from powdered lava
– of course originating from the volcano
of Mount Etna.

THE COSTANZO FAMILY

A palmento is an ancient wine-producing room where grapes are pressed and where the juice falls down using gravity only. Apart from the recently restored palmento, the Contanzo family has a modern cellar equipped with different sizes of oak barrels and oak egg-shaped vats. This white wine, however, ages six months on stainless steel tanks and another six months in the bottle before release.

Mimmo and Valeria Costanzo founded the winery in 2011. Their vines range in age from 30 to 120 years old. The Costanzo family farms organically on all of their ten hectares planted with vines. The steep vineyards are on terraces made from hardened lava stones.

Bianco di Sei

Palmento Costanzo

COOL VOLCANO WINE

Based on the island's location, you might expect a Sicilian wine to be sunny, warm and full-bodied. But anyone who has climbed the volcano understands why you can speak of a cool climate with wines originating from Mount Etna. This white wine is a blend of two local grape varieties: carricante and catarratto.

In terms of taste, this wine is all about a smashing acidity and mouthwatering bitters. Bianco di Sei is crisp and fresh with green apple, lemon and grapefruit bitters. Herbal with dill, mint, sage and basil, but also fennel and anise. Complex, precise and smoky, the wine is a perfect pairing with seafood or a green salad.

CARRICANTE AND CATARRATTO

Mount Etna is a magical place. From many places in Sicily, you can see the volcano, and often smoking. Etna is the most active volcano in Europe. The Parco dell'Etna is a national park and a UNESCO World Heritage Site. Because of its many eruptions, the soil around the volcano is very fertile. The subsoil, which is naturally rich in volcanic rock, gives the local grapes and their wines a special taste rich in minerality. On the northern flanks of the volcano, the black grapes nerello mascalese and nerello cappuccio grow plentifully, but also the white varieties carricante and catarratto.

These two grapes, often mistaken for each other, both originate from Sicily. Catarratto is the most frequently planted grape variety on the island and is also used for the fortified Marsala wines and for distillation purposes. Carricante is known for its high acidity and excellent quality. The local DOC prescribes that Etna Bianco contains at least 60% carricante. In the case of Bianco di Sei, the wine contains as much as 90% carricante.

CHATEAU
BARBEBELLE
ROSE FLEURI

AOC Coteaux d'Aix-en-Provence, France

OUR PROVINCE

The name Provence derives from classical antiquity, when the Romans were conquering Europe and Northern Africa. The French area that we nowadays know under the name of 'Provence' was indeed just a province of the huge Roman Empire. They used to call the region *Provincia Nostra* (our province).

Yes, they do make red and white in Provence, but we can all agree that rosé is the one thing that this region is all about. Of all the wine regions in the world, Provence is the one that is most specialised in rosé. Figures range from 75 to 88% of the total production. The key success factors of the Provence rosé are harvesting by night (and early in the morning), having short or even no skin contact with the grapes, and as little contact with oxygen during the vinification process as possible. The result is a pale pink rosé: light in colour, fresh, clean and energising.

BEAUTIFUL BEARD CASTLE

The label of the Rosé Fleuri contains a striking image. Is it a hipster? Is it a taste description? Is it an image of the estate name? Yes, it is all those things. Château Barbebelle (literally: Beautiful Beard Castle) sounds like a great modern marketing project, but in fact it has borne this name since the 16th century. The story goes that a former owner of the castle was a bearded gentleman, hence the name of the estate.

The Château Barbebelle wines did not always look like this, and in fact only the entry-level 'Fleuri' range (also available in white and red) is labelled with the bearded man. There are two other ranges available in rosé, white and red as well: the new Cuvée Héritage and the Cuvée Madeleine. The latter is named after the daughter of the château, the lovely Madeleine Premmereur.

Rosé Fleuri

Château Barbebelle

Madeleine Premmereur and her father Brice Herbeau

Château Barbebelle is based in Coteaux d'Aix-en-Provence, one of the nine sub-regions with an AOC status within Provence. Heading the company is the Herbeau family: Madeleine Premmereur (fourth generation) and her father are the current owners of the estate. Château Barbebelle is situated on a 300-hectare nature reserve, of which only 45 hectares are planted with vines. The vineyards of Château Barbebelle are among the oldest in Aix-en-Provence.

The white wines of the estate are made from the local grapes rolle, ugni blanc, sauvignon blanc and grenache blanc (only used for the Héritage range). But honestly, at this vineyard, it is all about the black grape varieties that are responsible not only for the reds, but more importantly for the rosé. Black grape varieties planted in the Château Barbebelle vineyards are grenache noir, syrah, cinsault and cabernet sauvignon.

BEWARE THE WOLF

The Château Barbebelle Rosé Fleuri is a blend of 50% grenache, 40% cinsault and 10% syrah. In taste you can discover tones of light red summer fruits such as strawberry, raspberry and pomegranate, as well as grapefruit, lemon, passion fruit and a hint of sweet harlequin roses. The wine is fruity, mineral and floral — just like the flowers in the beard of the hipster-bearded man who once owned the castle.

At first glance, this easy drinking rosé looks friendly, light and crisp — but it is a wolf in sheep's clothing. On the culinary spectrum, this wine is your summer companion that you will want to serve on a hot day, a perfect combination with local Provençal dishes such as salade niçoise or bouillabaisse. It's also the usual suspect to pair with your steak tartare or carpaccio. The wine has a dangerously high drinkability.

TOTH FERENC
EGRIBIKAVER

Eger, Hungary

BULL'S BLOOD

Egri Bikaver literally translates as 'the bull's blood from Eger'. This Hungarian wine-producing region named after its most important city has a story to tell with each and every wine. For this particular story, we have to go back to 1552. It was the year of the Siege of Eger: the successful resistance of a minority fighting a superior Turkish army.

The attacking Ottoman army consisted of 40,000 soldiers, bound and determined to conquer Eger Castle. A force of only 2,100 Hungarian soldiers, peasants and women defended this castle – an unequal battle, as you can imagine. And yet it was the Hungarians who won the Battle of Eger. Their secret weapon? A local red wine known today as Egri Bikavér.

RED BULL AVANT LA LETTRE

During the exhausting siege István Dobó, captain of the fortress of Eger, decided to open the castle's wine cellars and serve the local wines to his soldiers. These thirsty men eagerly drank the dark red wine, which they spilled in their beards and moustaches. Of course the alcohol in the wine had an effect on their behaviour, which made them fearless and without any kind of restraint.

For the Turks, however, all this was new. They drew the wrong conclusion after seeing their red beards and thought that the Hungarians drank bull's blood in order to give them extra strength and to make them outrageous. Their appearance was like a red rag to a bull. Today, Eger stands as a symbolic place to all Hungarians. It is a reminder of patriotic heroism. The red bull on the label of this wine is a symbol for the Siege of Eger.

Egri Bikavér

Eger Castle

THE CHATEAUNEUF-DU-PAPE OF HUNGARY

Eger is the first protected area of origin in Hungary. Since 1997, Eger has been a DHC, Districtus Hungaricus Controllatus, comparable to the Austrian DAC or the French AOC. The wine is always a blend of at least three grapes, including the local hero kékfrankos. The word kék means 'blue' in Hungarian, which will help you to remember that kékfrankos is the Hungarian equivalent of blaufränkisch.

Just like in Châteauneuf-du-Pape, Egri winemakers have the ability to use a total of 13 different grape varieties in their blend. The usual suspects are present and accounted for: merlot, cabernet sauvignon, cabernet franc, syrah and pinot noir. But the wine also includes less travelled varieties such as kadarka, bíborkadarka, blauer portugieser (kékoportó), blauburger, zweigelt, menoir and turán.

RED BEARDS AGAIN

The Tóth Ferenc Egri Bikavér is a blend of six different base wines made from kékfrankos, pinot noir, merlot, cabernet franc, kadarka and cabernet sauvignon. The wine spends 18 months on different sizes of oak barrels. This makes it intensely fruity, complex and medium-bodied, rich in spices and tannins.

Over the years, the blends of the Egri Bikavér wines have changed. Kékfrankos has always been the main variety, but kadarka and zweigelt grew in popularity during the country's Communist period. Most of the Hungarian wines were transported to the Soviet Union in those days, which caused the winemakers to prioritise quantity instead of quality. From the start of the DHC, Egri Bikavér wines have been back on track to be Hungary's most sought-after red wine. The focus on quality has been restored, making the wines stronger and darker — enough to make your beard look red again.

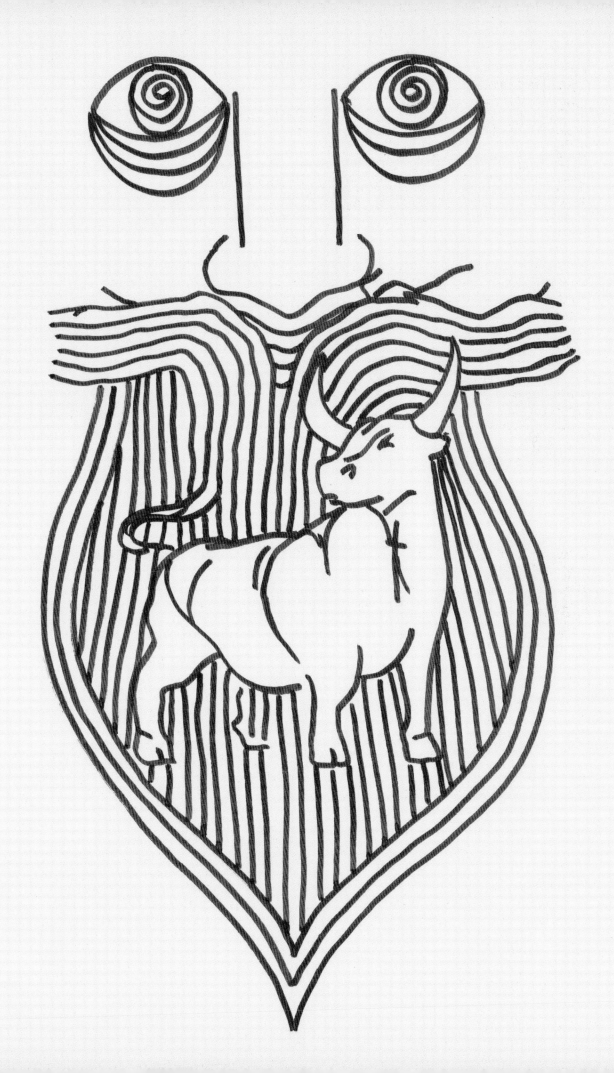

ACKNOWLEDGEMENTS

We would like to thank the wine producers that were brave enough to cooperate with us in the realisation of this book. Thank you for creating these wines, each of which is adorned with a label that tells a story, makes a statement, and stands out from the crowd.

Danny Griffioen, thanks for your beautiful analogue photography. Your images craft a wonderful story — perfect for our chapter navigation and for achieving a consistent line in the images of the bottles. Your work has ensured that this really has become the other wine book.

In addition, a word of thanks to Harold Hamersma, who has been a true motivator and mentor. Madeline Puckette, thank you for all your pioneering work in wine communication. Many thanks to Hugh Johnson and Jancis Robinson, who are always an inexhaustible source of wine knowledge.

We also want to thank the entire Fitzroy team, and in particular Stephanie Silonero, who was the driving force behind the whole operation. Without her, Burp would have remained nothing more than a good idea. Thank you, Eva van Lieshout, for your design and dedication. And of course Marnix Tiggeloven, owner of Fitzroy along with Jur. Thank you for believing in the book and giving us your trust, which resulted in the founding of Fitzroy Publishing.

We would also like to thank Joy Phillips for the linguistic finishing touches. During the making of this book, we received extra help from Wijnkoperij De Gouden Ton, David Bolomey and Joris Snelten. Thank you for that.

There may be errors in this book. Stories are passed on from one to the other. We are also aware that the rules and regulations of the local authorities of all the different wine regions in the world continue to change over time. As a result, information could be out of date. While making this book, we have tried to respect copyrights wherever possible.

When creating the illustrations, we tried to make people look real. However, all illustrations are drawn by hand with a marker and therefore only contain rough lines. We sincerely hope that we have not embarrassed anyone in how they are represented here.

The making of this book was a joy to do. As everyone knows, the world of wine is endless. The same may also apply to the making of Burp. Who knows? Perhaps in future there will be room for Burp the other wine book, Parts II, III, IV, V and VI. Just like Rocky.

Last but not least, we would like to thank Daniëlle Robben and Claartje Bakker. Where would we be without you?

Amsterdam, November 2020
Jur Baart & Bas Korpel

ISBN 978 90 6369 627 6

BIS Publishers
Borneostraat 80-A
1094 CP Amsterdam
The Netherlands
T +31 (0)20 515 02 30
bis@bispublishers.com
www.bispublishers.com

www.theotherwinebook.com

PREMIER JE SUIS

MOUTON NE CHANGE